FLASHBULB MEMORIES

Flashbulb Memories

Martin A. Conway
Department of Psychology,
University of Bristol

LAWRENCE ERLBAUM ASSOCIATES, PUBLISHERS
Hove (UK)   Hillsdale (USA)

Lawrence Erlbaum Associates Ltd, Publishers
27 Palmeira Mansions
Church Road
Hove
East Sussex, BN3 2FA
UK

British Library Cataloguing in Publication Data

A catalogue record for this book is available from the British Library

ISBN 0-86377-353-2
ISSN 0959-4779

Printed and bound by BPC Wheatons Ltd, Exeter

To Sue

Contents

Preface   ix

1. The Flashbulb Memory Hypothesis   1

The Flashbulb Analogy   3
Factors Influencing Flashbulb Memory Formation   4
The Flashbulb Memory Hypothesis   10

2. The Case Against Flashbulb Memories   17

Neisser's Critique   17
The *Challenger* Studies   27
Studies of Other Public Events: An Assassination, a War
    and a Public Disaster   38
Conclusions   41

3. Evidence for Flashbulb Memories   43

The Attempted Assassination of Ronald Reagan   43
The San Francisco Earthquake   49
The Resignation of Margaret Thatcher   53
Conclusions   66

4. **"Real" Flashbulb Memories and Flashbulb Memories Across the Lifespan   67**

Personal Flashbulb Memories   68
Traumatic Flashbulb Memories   76
Flashbulb Memories Across the Lifespan   81
Conclusions   92

5. **The Neurobiology of Flashbulb Memories   95**

Memory "Circuits"   96
Memory "Mechanisms"   103
Conclusions: Routes to Memory Formation   105

6. **Revising the Flashbulb Memory Hypothesis   109**

What are Flashbulb Memories?   110
What are the Conditions for Flashbulb Memory
    Formation?   114
Emotion, Importance and Plans   117
Functions of Flashbulb Memories   121
Conclusions: The Multifunctionality of Flashbulb
    Memories   126

References   129

Author Index   137

Subject Index   139

Preface

On the morning of 22 November 1990 (by a curious coincidence the 17th anniversary of the assassination of President John F. Kennedy), I was talking to a colleague, Dennis Hay, when my wife Susan Gathercole joined us. We were standing in the doorway of Dennis' office fairly excitedly discussing the rumour that the then British Prime Minister Margaret Thatcher had unexpectedly resigned. My memory now becomes a little confused because I know that other colleagues then joined us—Brenda Flude, and possibly Mary Smyth. Brenda went off to her office which was close by to call a friend for further details. I have a vivid recollection of standing in the doorway of her office a few moments later as she replaced the telephone receiver and confirmed that Thatcher's resignation had indeed been officially announced. I am sure that all of us in the corridor at that moment felt the heightened sense of awareness and slight feeling of unreality associated with the announcement of surprising and highly significant news—certainly these were my feelings.

Later that morning during a meeting with two of my graduate students, Stephen Anderson and Peter Hayes, I realised that this was one of those rare opportunities to conduct a flashbulb memory study—an opportunity that simply could not be missed by memory researchers interested in autobiographical memory. During the course of the meeting, it occurred to us that we could sample large groups by recruiting colleagues at other universities in the UK, in North America and in Denmark, to administer a standard flashbulb memory questionnaire to their students as part of a class exercise. We immediately started e-mailing and faxing our colleagues. The results of the studies that arose from that meeting led directly to the present volume. Along the way I learned that the study of flashbulb memories was far wider and more diverse than I had previously thought, and it became apparent to me that memory researchers had underestimated the prevalence of these highly detailed, durable and vivid memories. This book is partly an attempt to bring together the diversity of findings and to evaluate a particular model of the formation of flashbulb memories originally proposed by Brown and Kulik (1977). Colleagues who assisted in our own flashbulb memory studies are acknowledged in the text. However, I should like to thank in particular Peter Morris of the Department of Psychology at the University of Lancaster who, while head of department, provided the project with critical financial support which we could not have obtained from other sources in the time-scale available to us. As far as the present book is concerned, I am indebted to Susan Gathercole for the many illuminating discussions we have had about flashbulb memories. Her incisive comments shaped my thinking and thus shaped the book.

Martin Conway
April 1994

CHAPTER ONE

The Flashbulb Memory Hypothesis

In the 1970s two researchers, Roger Brown and James Kulik (1977), became interested in reports of surprisingly detailed and vivid memories for learning the news of certain prominent public events. The clarity and persistence of these memories were so striking that Brown and Kulik named them *flashbulb memories* (FMs). Informal evidence of the ubiquity of FMs emerged in an article from the popular magazine *Esquire* (1973), in which a number of celebrities recounted their memories of learning the news of the assassination of the American President John F. Kennedy that had occurred some 10 years prior to the *Esquire* interviews. What aroused Brown and Kulik's interest was not the fact that the celebrities were able to recall that JFK had indeed been assassinated, but rather that they also recalled, often in minute detail, their personal circumstances when learning of the assassination (see Yarmey & Bull, 1978, for a detailed study of JFK FMs). They remembered what they were doing, who they were with, where they were, and each account also contained a number of idiosyncratic details of the type that are usually rapidly and completely forgotten. In order to gain some perspective on the remarkable durability and specificity of FMs, consider the following memory accounts reported (and partly corroborated) in a recent Independent Television (ITV) programme on British television commemorating the 30th anniversary of JFK's assassination (*Where were you?*, ITV, 22 November 1993):

Terry Lancaster, Foreign Editor (1963), *Daily Express*:

I got to the foreign desk and found a scene of amazing confusion and tension. Now I'd given up smoking that day—I gave up smoking fairly frequently—so the moment that I heard that Kennedy was dead I took off my coat and sent my secretary out for three packets of cigarettes.

Ludovick Kennedy, Writer and Broadcaster:

I was on my way home from the studios at Lime Grove and I had the wireless on and I heard this announcement, which was breaking into whatever programme was on, that he'd [JFK] been shot and I remember as I heard those words I said aloud, I was quite alone in the car, I said aloud "Oh no, Oh, no".

Gerry Anderson, Film Producer:

I was with my ex-wife in a West End cinema when I became aware of something going on behind me and I turned round and I could see people in the back row of the balcony chatting busily to each other and even talking to the people in the row in front of them and I guessed that something pretty dreadful had happened—and you know the way today at football matches people create the "human wave" which moves across the stadium? Well in the same way the ripple came down the balcony and eventually I said to the man behind me "What's happened?", and he said "Kennedy's been assassinated".

And for an account which is strikingly detailed, possibly because of the intersection of the news with the rememberer's ongoing interests at the time:

Derek Waken, Teacher:

I finished teaching about 4 o'clock and I thought between 4 and 6 I would take some cadets shooting on the range. So we went up with at least 4 if not 8 cadets and a captain of shooting, a young chap called Cameron Kennedy, and against all the rules I asked him if he'd lock up so I gave him the armoury keys, the magazine keys, and the ammunition and I left because the next day was Saturday and there was going to be a film so I thought I'll thread up the first spool now. Suddenly one of the auditorium doors opened, light flooded in and a small boy standing there in silhouette shouted "Sir, Sir, Kennedy's been shot!". With that he disappeared. Then I switched off the light and set off rather slowly, could have been thinking about alibis I suppose, set off slowly for the sort of Matron's area of the school, and I didn't like to ask her directly and so I said "Matron, is there anything I should know?", and she said "Yes, President Kennedy's been shot". Whereupon the weight was off me, I'd got my job back, and I was extremely happy.

These memories retained over a 30-year period and the memories reported in the *Esquire* article are unusual on three counts. First, they preserve knowledge of personal circumstances when learning of a public occurrence. Second, they are highly detailed and feature knowledge of minutiae not present in most autobiographical memories associated with news events (Larsen, 1992). Third, the memories endure in apparently unchanged form for many years. In order to account for these unusual memories, Brown and Kulik (1977) conducted their own investigation into FMs and developed a model of the function and formation of FMs—the *flashbulb memory hypothesis* (FMH). The purpose of this initial chapter is simply to describe Brown and Kulik's (1977) original findings and to outline the FMH. Later chapters examine criticisms of the FMH, appraise subsequent studies, examine FMs arising from personal experiences rather than public events, and review current neurological findings relating to FM formation. The closing chapter assesses how the FMH has fared in the face of fairly persistent criticism and how it might be developed to encompass the broader range of current findings.

THE FLASHBULB ANALOGY

Brown and Kulik (1977) introduced the term "flashbulb" memories to convey the notion that these types of memories preserve knowledge of an event in an almost indiscriminate way—rather as a photograph preserves all the details of a scene. However, Brown and Kulik did not intend that the analogy between FMs and photographs be taken literally. Instead, they argued that although FMs often featured the recall of minutiae, they were, nonetheless, incomplete records of experienced events. Indeed, rather than emphasising the completeness of FMs, Brown and Kulik drew attention to what they called the "live" quality of FMs, in which only some perceptual and other details of an event come to mind with great vividness and clarity. In order to illustrate both the clarity and the incompleteness of FMs, Brown and Kulik provided descriptions of their own memories for learning of JFK's assassination:

> I was on the telephone with Miss Johnson, the Dean's secretary, about some departmental business. Suddenly, she broke in with: "Excuse me a moment: everyone is excited about something. What? Mr Kennedy has been shot!" We hung up, I opened my door to hear further news as it came in, and then

resumed my work on some forgotten business that "had to be finished" that day (Brown).

I was seated in a sixth-grade music class, and over the intercom I was told that the president had been shot. At first, everyone just looked at each other. The class started yelling, and the music teacher tried to calm everyone down. About ten minutes later I heard over the intercom that Kennedy had died and that everyone should return to their homeroom. I remember that when I got to my homeroom my teacher was crying and everyone was standing in a state of shock. They told us to go home (Kulik).

These accounts clearly convey the "live" quality, high definition and clarity of the memories from which they are derived. They also illustrate, however, the incomplete nature of the underlying memories (e.g. the forgotten departmental business in Brown's account) and as Brown and Kulik (1977, p. 75) point out, other details such as the teacher's dress in Kulik's memory are also not available. Thus, FMs, although unusually clear and detailed, differ from photographs in that they do not indiscriminately preserve all the features of an event but, as we shall see, they do preserve certain common event features.

FACTORS INFLUENCING FLASHBULB MEMORY FORMATION

In order to investigate how FMs are formed, Brown and Kulik (1977) conducted the first formal FM study. They started with two intuitions. The first, based on the JFK assassination, was that the public event had to be unexpected and novel and, therefore, surprising. The second was that different events would vary in their consequentiality or significance for different sub-groups within society. For instance, the assassination of the civil rights campaigner Martin Luther King was certainly consequential for Black North Americans and so should be associated with a high frequency of FMs in this group. Brown and Kulik suspected that this event would be less consequential for White North Americans and, accordingly, that there would be a lower frequency of FMs in this group. For their study, Brown and Kulik selected nine surprising public events, some of which they assumed would vary in consequentiality for Black and White groups of subjects and others which should have the same effect for both groups. The nine events were: the assassinations of Medgar Evers, John F. Kennedy, Malcolm X, Martin Luther King and Robert Kennedy, the attempted assassinations of George Wallace and Gerald Ford, the scandal associated with Ted Kennedy, and the death of General Francisco Franco. A tenth event required recall of a private event featuring an unexpected personal shock.

In Brown and Kulik's study, subjects answered "Yes" or "No" to the question "Do you recall the circumstances in which you first heard that ...?" (obviously the wording of this question was changed slightly for the tenth "personal" event). When subjects answered "Yes", they were then required to write an account of their memory and this could take any form and be of any length. Note that following Larsen (1992), memory for one's personal circumstances when learning of an item of news will, hereafter, be referred to as memory for the *reception event*. Memory for a reception event should not be conflated with memory for an actual item of news and this is because the representation of public events in long-term memory (cf. Brown, 1990) differs from that for reception events. After describing each reception event, the subjects then rated the consequentiality of the item of news on a 5-point scale, where a 1 indicated "little or no consequentiality for me" and a 5 indicated "very high consequentiality for me". For this rating of consequentiality, each subject was instructed to judge the consequentiality of the event for his or her *own* life. Specifically, they were instructed: "Probably the best single question to ask yourself in rating consequentiality is '*What* consequences for my life, both direct and indirect, has this event had?' " (Brown & Kulik, 1977, p. 82). They were further instructed to consider how things might have gone, in their own lives, if the original event had *not* occurred. Brown and Kulik emphasise that they devoted considerable effort in communicating to subjects that it was the *personal* consequentiality or *personal* importance of the news item that should be assessed and not its wider national, international or historical significance. Finally, subjects also estimated their overt rehearsal of the memories and rated, on a 4-point scale, how frequently they had given an account of each reception event: "never told anyone", "gave the same account 1 to 5 times", "gave the same account 6 to 10 times", "gave the same account more than 10 times".

In order to score the memory descriptions of the various reception events, Brown and Kulik studied a subset of the accounts and developed a coding scheme that they then independently applied to the whole set. In developing the coding scheme, they identified six categories of information that were common to the memories in their sample and these were *place*, *ongoing event*, *informant*, *affect in others*, *own affect* and *aftermath*. In the case of memory accounts relating a personal unexpected shock, the category *affect in others* was rarely present, although all the other categories were present as were four new categories: *event*, *person*, *cause* and *time*. These additional categories specify information implicit in the other nine events. So pervasive were the categories of *place*, *ongoing event*, *informant*, *affect in others*, *own affect* and *aftermath* that Brown and Kulik referred to them as the "canonical" categories of recall. Using this coding scheme, an event was classified as a FM if the subject answered

"Yes" to the initial question and then provided detailed information on one or more of the canonical categories. When the authors then independently classified the memory accounts and the separate classifications were compared, a high degree of consensus was observed with exact agreement on 90% of the classifications.

Before turning to a full account of Brown and Kulik's findings, it is worth noting the type of information in the FM descriptions. This information was highly detailed and, although classed within one of the six general canonical categories, was specific to individual subjects, for example having a conversation with a classmate at Shaw University, talking to a woman friend on the telephone, having dinner in a French restaurant, and so on. Many of the accounts also included idiosyncratic event features which did not fit any of the canonical categories but that nonetheless demonstrated the fine grain of memory details in FMs. For example, comments such as "the weather was cloudy and grey", "she said 'Oh God! I knew they would kill him'", "we all had on our little blue uniforms", and "I was carrying a carton of Viceroy cigarettes which I dropped", constitute a type of highly specific event detail rarely present in memory for most news events and, indeed, comparatively infrequent in everyday autobiographical memories (for reviews of, and recent findings in, autobiographical memory, see Conway, 1990; in press; Conway & Rubin, 1993; Conway, Rubin, Spinnler, & Wagenaar, 1992; Rubin, 1986; in press). These idiosyncratic event details lend support to Brown and Kulik's claim that FMs have a "live" quality.

What then of the incidence of FMs across the subject groups for the different items of news? Figure 1.1 shows the proportions of subjects classified as having FMs to the various news events. The incidence of FMs across groups differed on only four of the events and the frequency of FMs was significantly higher for Blacks than Whites for the murders of Medgar Evers, Malcolm X and Martin Luther King, and the attempted murder of George Wallace. For the first three of these events, the differences are marked. For instance, none of the Whites could recall the reception event in which they learned of the news of the murder of Medgar Evers, only one White had a FM for the murder of Malcolm X, and although a third of the Whites had FMs for the murder of Martin Luther King, this was far less than the Blacks, three-quarters of whom had FMs for this event. This aspect of the findings fits well with Brown and Kulik's proposal that the personal consequentiality of an item of news is an important precondition to the formation of FMs. Further evidence for this was also present in the ratings of personal consequentiality of each news item and mean consequentiality ratings across groups are shown in Fig. 1.2.

It can be seen from Fig. 1.2 that Blacks rated the murders of Medgar Evers, Malcolm X and Martin Luther King, and the attempted murder of George Wallace, higher in personal consequences than Whites and these

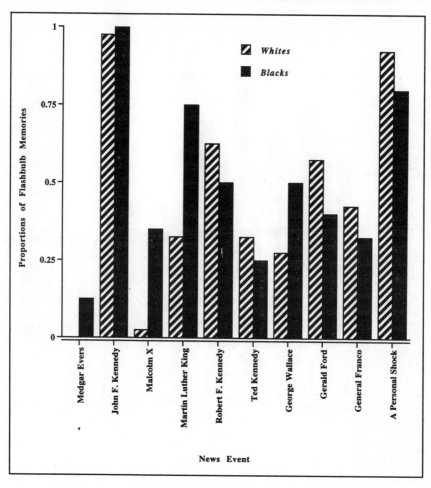

FIG. 1.1. Frequency of flashbulb memories to 10 events (data from Brown & Kulik, 1977, table 2).

differences were found to be reliable. Although a higher incidence of FMs and higher consequentiality for Blacks than Whites to learning the news of the murders of Medgar Evers, Malcolm X and Martin Luther King were expected, the same pattern of differences for the attempted murder of George Wallace, a right-wing white politician, appears slightly unusual. However, as Brown and Kulik point out, Governor Wallace's far-right stance on civil rights and racial issues made him a more significant figure for the Blacks than the Whites and the consequences of his retirement from the political arena would undoubtedly have been more consequential for Blacks than Whites. Thus, the incidence of FMs to the news of the

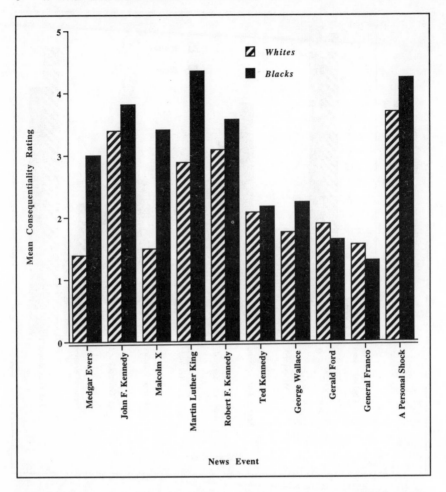

FIG. 1.2. Mean consequentiality ratings for 10 events (data from Brown & Kulik, 1977, table 3).

attempted assassination of George Wallace also fits well with the consequentiality hypothesis.

Of the other events shown in Fig. 1.1, it is clear that the assassination of JFK gave rise to the highest incidence of FMs and in both groups virtually all subjects were classified as having FMs for learning the news of this assassination. The JFK event was of equally high significance for both groups (see Fig. 1.2) and lead to the widespread formation of FMs. It is, however, interesting to note that for the Black group, the assassination of the civil rights leader Martin Luther King was rated as more consequential than JFK and for both groups memory for a personal surprising and shocking event lead to the highest consequentiality ratings. We will return to these points in Chapter 4. The remaining events shown in Fig. 1.1 were associated with variable frequencies of FMs and produced no systematic differences between the two groups. FMs to these events may, perhaps, have depended on the intersection of the actual news item with the specific interests of individual subjects. So, for example, a person concerned with European politics may have found the death of General Franco to be consequential and, accordingly, a FM was formed. In contrast, for other subjects with few specific interests in this area, consequentiality may have been low and so no FMs were formed.

Brown and Kulik also measured overt rehearsal of FMs and Fig. 1.3 shows the percentage of overt rehearsals greater than zero, for memories for which this measure was available. Note that for each event, data from different numbers of subjects were used according to whether or not a subject had in fact recalled a FM to the event (see Brown & Kulik, 1977, tables 4 and 5). Comparing Fig. 1.3 with Fig. 1.2 it can be seen that rehearsal and consequentiality vary in similar ways and this correlation was found to be significant for Whites but not for Blacks. Thus there is some evidence that consequentiality and rehearsal are related.

Finally, Fig. 1.4 shows the mean number of content or canonical categories featured in each FM account (maximum score is 6 and data for the "personal shock" event are not shown). Across both groups and all events, most subjects spontaneously provided information on two to three canonical categories and for the JFK event the average was four or more. Thus, the canonical categories of location, activity, informant, etc., were a common and general feature of the FM descriptions. It was also found that ratings of consequentiality were highly correlated with the number of canonical categories, which suggests that this variable is not only central to FM formation but may also help determine the actual content of FMs.

In summary, there are a number of seminal findings from Brown and Kulik's study concerning the frequency and formation of FMs. First, and perhaps foremost, public events that are high in personal consequentiality or personal importance are associated with a high incidence of FMs. This is shown by the widespread occurrence of FMs to the assassination of JFK and by the systematic and reliable variations in FM frequency for Blacks and Whites to news events of different group saliency. Second, both public and private events that are surprising and shocking are associated with high rates of FMs. Third, FMs contain some general categories of knowledge (the "canonical" categories) and often feature the vivid retention of event minutiae. Fourth, and finally, rates of overt rehearsal are correlated to some extent with consequentiality and memory content. In later chapters, we will evaluate the extent to which subsequent studies have been able to corroborate these four core findings.

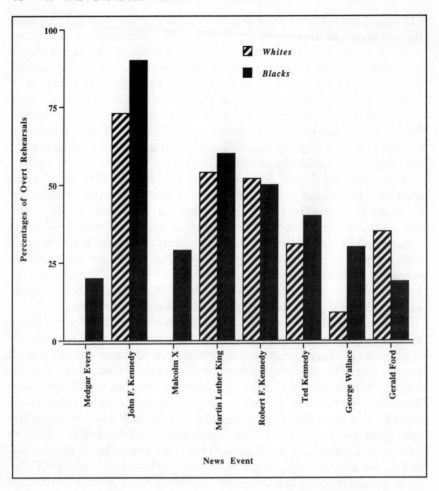

FIG. 1.3. Mean consequentiality ratings for 8 events (data from Brown & Kulik, 1977, table 4).

THE FLASHBULB MEMORY HYPOTHESIS

In order to account for their findings, Brown and Kulik proposed an *encoding* account of FM formation. According to this account, processes occurring at or close to the reception event initiate the creation of FMs. Figure 1.5 shows a flow chart of how the proposed processes operate over time. In response to a stimulus event (i.e. news of a public occurrence), some degree of surprise is assigned and experienced. In cases of extreme surprise, the whole memory system may be destabilised resulting in amnesia for the event. In contrast, when an event is routine and unsurprising, it is

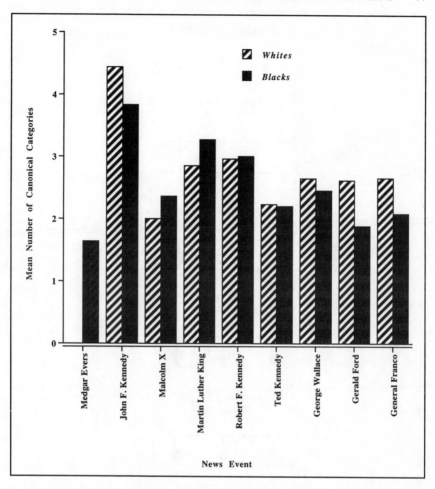

FIG. 1.4. Mean number of canonical categories for flashbulb memories to 9 events (data from Brown & Kulik, 1977, table 5).

not focally attended to and no detailed memory is formed. However, when the surprise value of an event falls between these two extremes, then a potential for FM formation is present. After determining the surprise value of an event, an assessment is then made of personal consequentiality or importance. If the event is judged low in personal consequentiality forgetting occurs, but if the event is personally relevant a FM is formed. (Note that the processes leading to the assignment of surprise and consequentiality values are assumed to be automatic and not under direct conscious control.) It is important to note, then, that according to the FMH, high values of *both* surprise and consequentiality are required if FMs are to be formed.

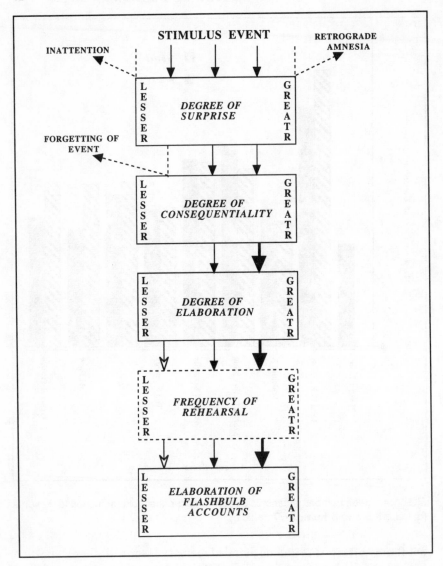

FIG. 1.5. Processing stages in flashbulb memory formation (after Brown & Kulik, 1977, fig. 1).

Once the process of FM formation has been initiated, then the actual degree of elaboration of a memory is determined by the level of personal consequentiality alone (Fig. 1.5). Thus, Brown and Kulik postulated that FMs themselves could vary in clarity and detail, and that this variation was positively correlated with personal consequentiality such that the greater the personal significance of the event the more clear and detailed the memory. This particular aspect of the FMH has often been overlooked and a corollary of it is that by no means all FMs will, for instance, contain information on all canonical categories. The interaction between surprise and consequentiality serves, then, to initiate FM formation, whereas the degree of consequentiality determines the elaborateness of the resulting FM.

Brown and Kulik made a strong distinction between a FM and an *account* derived from a FM. According to this aspect of the FMH, the generation of accounts and the possible encoding in memory of those accounts is separate from FM formation and representation in long-term memory. The number of accounts associated with a FM is determined, in part, by degree of consequentiality, and highly consequential news items lead to multiple accounts of the reception event. Brown and Kulik argued that accounts of FMs do not change the actual FM memory in any way, which, they suggested, was probably non-verbal and had to be accessed and then processed further in order to generate a verbal account or description. When an account itself was stored in long-term memory, then this acted to provide a further source of cues with which to access the unchanging and durable FM formed at encoding. (In Chapter 6, this somewhat circular aspect of the FMH is examined further.) In this model rehearsal, in the form of recounting an event, is influenced by the significance of the event for the individual and different accounts are developed during separate episodes of rehearsal.

The encoding account of FM formation shown in Fig. 1.5 constitutes Brown and Kulik's cognitive theory of the genesis of FMs. Brown and Kulik, however, went on to outline a potential neuroanatomical theory of FM formation based on the work of Livingston (1967a; 1967b; see Chapter 5). Livingston proposed that FMs arise through the action of the limbic and reticular systems. Structures in the reticular formation respond to novelty (surprise) and other structures in the limbic system evaluate the "biological" significance of an event. When the "biological" significance of an event passes some criterion, the limbic system discharges into the reticular system, which responds with a diffuse discharge distributed throughout the cortical hemispheres. This interaction of limbic and reticular systems causes a memory to be formed of all recent brain events above a certain level of organisation—Livingston called the discharge into the hemispheres a "Now Print!" command. For Brown and Kulik, Livingston's model provided a plausible neuroanatomical mechanism for FM formation and their measure of consequentiality was intended to provide an index of "biological significance".

Brown and Kulik argued that the evolution of the "Now Print!" encoding mechanism predated the emergence of human society and the development of skills such as writing. They proposed that the "Now Print!" device delivered an evolutionary advantage by giving rise to very specific and durable memories of events of high personal consequence. Such memories might be used vicariously in preparing effective avoidance and approach strategies and so aid survival. Clearly, in the absence of external records of experienced events, a "Now Print!" device would serve an evolutionary purpose and continue to function long after the emergence of more permanent independent records. Thus, in prehistory, FMs constituted records of experienced events that facilitated survival and, in the present age, continue to provide detailed memories of events which although high in personal consequentiality are, perhaps, less directly related to individual survival.

There are two aspects to the FMH which require further comment, one relating to FM content and the other to accuracy. According to the "Now Print!" theory, a record of all recent brain events *above a certain level of organisation* is recorded. The question is what is this "level of organisation"? It seems unlikely that this could be, for example, a fine-grain level at which all specific and dedicated sequences of processes currently executing during the reception event were encoded into a memory. Indeed, we have already seen that FMs do not indiscriminately preserve all event details. On the other hand, the idiosyncratic details in FMs often seem to reflect exactly this fine-grain of detail. Consider, for instance, the colleague who informed Brown and Kulik that he could still feel the special rubber tread of the steps he happened to be walking on when informed of the assassination of JFK. FMs, then, contain some highly detailed fine-grain knowledge and some course-grain, more general knowledge (the canonical categories of place, activity, others, etc.). Thus, a reasonable inference from Brown and Kulik's account is that FMs represent both specific details of, and conceptual knowledge relating to, a reception event. In short, FMs represent the meaning and structure of a reception event contextualised by the retention of event minutiae. The "level of organisation", then, is semantic, and the recipient's prior knowledge, goals and orientation to the news must undoubtedly be of central importance in FM formation.

One of the most intriguing aspects of Brown and Kulik's paper relates to an interesting omission—the word "accuracy" is never used. We will see in Chapter 2 that the accuracy of FMs has become a central issue for the FMH and it is fairly obvious why this should be—or so it seems at first glance. If FMs arise from processes occurring at encoding, then it follows that FMs should constitute an accurate record of event details. There are, however, problems with this inference. First, FMs are not complete records of a reception event and, therefore, cannot be fully accurate in the sense that they maintain a veridical record of all event details. Second, the notion of "accuracy" is itself problematic and this was at least hinted at by Brown and Kulik in their proposal that only event details "above a certain level of organisation" are retained in FMs. The problem is that as an event is experienced, the individual has an evolving model of the meaning of the unfolding event and, possibly, it is this model that is retained in memory. The event model will direct attention during experience and determine the interpretation placed upon event details. Memory for an event model might then be highly accurate, it might even be a veridical record of the original model, but it does not follow that the original model was a veridical record of the actual event. Indeed, the original model is a complex and dynamic *interpretation* of an experienced event. Brown and Kulik's focus on different groups of subjects and the perceived consequentiality of different news items shows, perhaps, some sensitivity to this problem of accuracy.

In summary, the two critically important points of the FMH are that a reception event must feature news that is *both* surprising and personally consequential if a FM is to be formed. The elaborateness of the resulting FM is determined by the degree of personal consequentiality and this must inevitably entail the prior knowledge of the rememberer and the extent to which the news is self-referring. FMs are not complete accounts of events and although they feature some highly specific, fine-grained, event knowledge, they also contain other more conceptual and abstract knowledge—they are memories of event-specific personal interpretations of unique and often unusual experiences. Finally, the FMH proposes that there are particular neuroanatomical sites and pathways that mediate FM formation and these brain circuits support the privileged encoding of FMs compared with other, more mundane memories.

CHAPTER TWO

The Case Against
Flashbulb Memories

Neisser (1982), in a critical appraisal of Brown and Kulik (1977), argued that most of the assumptions of the FMH were either wrong or questionable. Instead, Neisser proposed an alternative theory that could account for both Brown and Kulik's data and for other FM findings. The first part of this chapter reviews Neisser's criticisms of Brown and Kulik and the second part evaluates recent studies that have been critical of the FMH.

NEISSER'S CRITIQUE

Neisser (1982) criticised the FMH on four counts—accuracy, encoding, consequentiality and content—and he also queried Brown and Kulik's evolutionary account of the function of FMs. On accuracy Neisser argued that at least some FMs may not be accurate and, therefore, such FMs could not have been formed by the actions of a special encoding mechanism. Instead, Neisser proposed that FMs were produced by frequent rehearsal which spontaneously occurred when a reception event was thought and talked about. As regards consequentiality, Neisser claimed that consequentiality was assigned *after* rather than during an event and so could not be the critical factor in FM formation. And for surprise he argued that high levels of arousal were associated with a narrowing of attention which clearly would not be conducive to encoding an event in detail. The concept of canonical categories constituting the fundamental categories of memory was also criticised, and Neisser suggested that these actually reflected narrative conventions of discourse rather than invariant features of memories. Finally, it is argued that the functions of FMs lie in promoting the integration of individuals with their society and not in adaptive functions with survival value. These criticisms, if correct, are devastating for Brown and Kulik's position and compel the outright rejection of the FMH. In this section, Neisser's critique is itself appraised and each of the four main points are evaluated individually as is the alternative account of the function of FMs.

Accuracy

One implication of the FMH is that FMs should, in general, be accurate accounts of events and this is because they are formed at the time of, or close in time to, the reception event. It was pointed out earlier that there is some ambiguity in the notion of accuracy, that is, whether accuracy refers to the actual details of an event or to an individual's on-line interpretation of an event. But in either case, FMs should be basically accurate representations of an event. After all, on-line cognitive models must, themselves, represent reality if events are to be responded to appropriately. To the extent that cases of strikingly inaccurate FMs can be identified, then this will obviously question one of the central proposals of the FMH—that FMs are formed by processes operating at encoding. Fundamentally inaccurate FMs cannot arise solely from encoding processes and must, therefore, necessarily entail processes operating after encoding. By this argument, the FMH could not apply to all FMs and consequently would require either rejection or considerable modification. One of Neisser's main criticisms of Brown and Kulik was that they had taken at face value the FM accounts provided by their subjects and assumed that they were basically accurate memories. Is this assumption warranted? Consider the two FM accounts below. In the first the film director Bunuel (1985) recalls the marriage of the artist Paul Nizan, and in the second Johnson (1985) recalls a family outing:

> The church of St-Germaine-des-Pre, where he was married, is crystal clear in my mind's eye. I can see the congregation, myself among them, the altar, the priest—even Jean-Paul Sartre, the best man. And then suddenly, one day last year, I said to myself—but that's impossible! Nizan, a militant Marxist, and his wife, who came from a family of agnostics, would never have been married in a church! It was categorically unthinkable. Did I make it up? Confuse it with other weddings? Did I graft a church I know well onto a story that someone told me? Even today I've no idea what the truth is. . .
> (Bunuel, 1985, p. 5)

My family was driving through the San Joaquin Valley in California when we had a flat tire. We didn't have a spare, so my father took the tire off the car and hitchhiked up the road to a gas station to get the tire patched. My mother, brother, sister, and I waited in the car. The temperature was over 100 degrees, extremely uncomfortable, and we got very thirsty. Finally, my sister took a couple of empty pop bottles and walked up the road to a farmhouse. The woman who lived there explained to her that the valley was suffering from a drought and she only had a little bottled-water left. She set aside a glass of water for her little boy, who would be home from school soon, and filled up my sister's pop bottles with the rest. My sister brought the water back to the car and we drank it. I also remembered feeling guilty that we didn't save any for my father, who would probably be thirsty when he got back with the repaired tire. (Johnson, 1985, p. 1)

Both of these FMs are incorrect. Bunuel's memory appears to involve some sort of reconstruction of where the wedding took place. Possibly, the exact location was not retained in the original FM and the reconstruction was added as an account was elaborated over a number of overt rehearsals. On the other hand, Bunuel could simply be wrong—maybe Nizan did marry in a church. The error in Johnson's memory was, however, verified by her parents, who confirmed that although the car trip and breakdown both occurred the water incident had not. Johnson (1985) argued that as she waited in the hot car she may have fantasised the water incident, and that this fantasy became integrated with her memory of the actual event with the consequence that the fantasy and the event could not be distinguished in her memory. Bunuel's memory clearly is a problem for the FMH, as it appears to involve some type of reconstruction occurring after encoding. Johnson's memory, on the other hand, is less of a problem if it is accepted that FMs are veridical records of an individual's on-line interpretation of events (i.e. what should or could have happened, as well as what did happen). Yet interesting though these cases are, they do not constitute a critical test of the FMH and this is because the personal consequentiality and surprise value of the events are unknown. If the events were not surprising and were not above some critical level of personal importance, then FM formation would not have occurred and, rather like many memories of everyday events (see Brewer, 1988; White, 1982), these two memories would feature forgetting and reconstruction.

More pressing are cases of what Neisser and Harsch (1992) termed "phantom flashbulbs" of events which were both surprising and consequential. For example, Linton (1975) reported the following FM for the assassination of JFK:

When I'm reminded of that date, particularly by you, I remember that you were the one who told me about the assassination ... I know that you came down and told me about what you ... had heard on the news. I don't know what time it was. Because down in the hole in F —————Hall one tended to lose track of time ... I had been working for some extended period of time and I was very much concentrating on what I was doing when I was interrupted by you having heard something about it. You said, I'm sure it was you who said, "The President has been assassinated, or shot". And I probably looked up and said, "What?" and you said "Kennedy, he's been shot". And I said "What do you mean? Where?" and you said you didn't know. (Linton, 1975, p. 387)

But Linton had no memory of this event and was able to establish, using verifiable external sources, that she could not have been the bearer of the news as she was not present at this location at the appropriate time. A clear case then of an apparently inaccurate FM for an event that certainly was surprising. But as the personal consequentiality of the JFK assassination for the rememberer is not known, it remains possible that this memory was not a FM simply because it may have been low in personal significance.

However, one of the most striking (and most commented upon) of phantom FMs of an event that certainly was surprising and personally consequential for the rememberer was reported by Neisser himself:

For many years I have remembered how I heard the news of the Japanese attack on Pearl Harbor, which occurred on the day before my thirteenth birthday. I recall sitting in the living room of our house—we only lived in that house for one year, but I remember it well—listening to a baseball game on the radio. The game was interrupted by an announcement of the attack, and I rushed upstairs to tell my mother. This memory has been so clear for so long that I never confronted its inherent absurdity until last year: no one broadcasts baseball games in December. (Neisser, 1982, p. 45)

This, then, would seem to be a definite case of a confabulated FM that clearly cannot be accounted for by the FMH. In fact, Neisser argued, mainly on the basis of this memory, that the encoding account of FM formation must be incorrect. Instead, he proposed that FMs were formed *after* encoding and it is only during thinking and talking about the reception event "later that day, the next day, and in subsequent months and years" (Neisser, 1982, p. 45) that a stable "memory" gradually emerges. We will return to Neisser's rehearsal theory of FM formation later in the chapter, but at this point let us consider the extent of the "incorrectness" of Neisser's Pearl Harbor FM.

How inaccurate can a memory be? It would surely be unusual, and it would undoubtedly have been detected by now, if there were a high incidence of *totally* fabricated FMs (but see Loftus, 1993). Indeed, previously, such fantastic fabrications have mainly been observed in patients with brain damage, and especially in patients with damage to the frontal lobes (Baddeley & Wilson, 1986; Shallice, 1988; Stuss & Benson, 1984). Thus, it seems unlikely that Neisser's memory could have been wholly confabulated—although it should be noted that Bunuel's memory of Nizan's wedding certainly seems like a candidate for the "fantastic confabulation" category and, therefore, such "memories" may not only arise through brain dysfunction. What seems more probable in relation to Neisser's memory is that it is basically correct with some erroneous detail added, possibly during the process of rehearsal. Thompson and Cowan (1986), through a serendipitous finding, were able to confirm that this was indeed the case.

Thompson and Cowan (1986) report an interview with the sports broadcaster Red Barber in which Barber described how, many years earlier, he had been commentating on a special Army *vs* Navy football game that was interrupted by the news of the Japanese attack on Pearl Harbor. Barber stated that:

> I was at the Polo Ground to scout the New York Giants who had already won the eastern division and were to play the Chicago Bears in two weeks for the championship. I was to broadcast that game. The Giants were playing the old NFL football Dodgers. At halftime, Lou Effrat of the *New York Times* came down from the press box and said Pearl Harbor had been bombed by Japan. I got up and went home. I was sick.

Even more remarkably, the two football teams had the same names as baseball teams and the match was played at a famous baseball ground. Thompson and Cowan (1986) concluded that Neisser's memory was largely accurate and contained only a minor error in reconstruction—the confusion of a football commentary with a baseball commentary. Neisser (1986), in his response to Thompson and Cowan (1986), agreed that he must have been listening to the football match referred to by Red Barber but pointed out that the particular reconstructive error he had made, the substitution of a baseball for a football match, was in itself significant. He argued that as a child of immigrant parents he had been eager to identify with his adopted culture and that during his childhood baseball was the "all American" game, whereas football was a comparatively recent professional sport. Neisser concluded that his reconstructive error reflected the influence of the self upon memory and demonstrated how memory details can become distorted in favour of the self (see Ross, 1989).

In terms of the FMH, there are a number of interpretations of Neisser's Pearl Harbor FM. Neisser's own interpretation is that it demonstrates the reconstructive nature of memory and could not have arisen through the operation of a special encoding device. An alternative to this is that the memory is in fact a FM formed in response to surprising and personally consequential news. There is, however, no reason to suppose that the FM would necessarily feature specific information about the content of the interrupted radio broadcast. Just as Brown had been on the telephone to the Dean's secretary about some "forgotten" business when learning of JFK's assassination (see Chapter 1), so Neisser may have failed to encode the specific content of the radio broadcast. Perhaps all that was encoded was the fact that a radio broadcast of a sports programme had been interrupted. If this were the case, then Neisser's FM for learning of the news of the Japanese attack upon Pearl Harbor could not be taken as evidence against the FMH, which actually predicts variation in the completeness of FMs. What is important from the perspective of the FMH, is the existence of a detailed and specific memory for the reception of this news event. Accounts derived from this memory will vary and, perhaps, some compensation for lack of detail relating to specific aspects of the event will be introduced into an account, much as Neisser (1986) suggested. But this does not exclude the possibility that a FM was originally formed at encoding and the reconstruction added later (see Chapter 6).

Another and more intriguing interpretation is that the reconstructive error was not introduced during rehearsal. Consider Neisser's (1986) argument that as a child he had a strong interest in baseball but only a marginal interest in football. Presumably, listening to a baseball rather than a football match would have been optimum and it is perhaps not too speculative to suggest that a young baseball enthusiast having to make do with a football broadcast might have imagined, fantasised or even wished that the broadcast was of a baseball rather than a football match. The resulting FM memory, formed when the news of the attack was announced, may not have distinguished between the wished for broadcast and the actual broadcast. Neisser's FM might then be similar to the FM described by Johnson (1985; see Chapter 1) and so constitute a failure of source monitoring at encoding rather than a perseverative reconstructive error in retrieval. If this were the case, then the Pearl Harbor FM would, again, support rather than question the FMH.

Instructive though these single "case" studies are, they do not, ultimately, constitute a serious challenge to the FMH. In general, little is known about the critical factors of surprise and personal consequentiality associated with the various items of news and the consistency and accuracy of the memories usually cannot be checked. The case studies do, however, bring the issue of accuracy into focus and it would seem, on balance, that even isolated FMs singled out as paradigm cases of inaccurate memories may not be as critical for the FMH as originally claimed.

Encoding

Having concluded that FMs are reconstructions rather than accurate records, Neisser (1982) then considered the emergence of such reconstructions. He proposed that FMs arise during the process of rehearsal which spontaneously and naturally occurs as we think and converse about learning surprising and consequential news. During these overt and covert rehearsals, a "story" or narrative gradually evolves, presumably becoming progressively more and more finely honed until some sort of core narrative is created which can then be used to generate a diverse number of accounts appropriate to many different types of audience. It is during the development of a narrative that reconstructive errors are incorporated into a "memory", whereas the main effect of the repeated rehearsals themselves is to promote the formation of a stable and durable long-term memory representation.

The suggestion that processes mediating rehearsal, rather than processes present during encoding, underlie FM formation is Neisser's strongest challenge to the FMH. The issue of encoding versus rehearsal can be resolved by empirical findings and, for the FMH, situations in which there was a high incidence of FMs with little or no associated rehearsal would clearly favour the encoding account. Similarly, findings that showed encoding factors to be more strongly associated with FMs than rehearsal rates would also support the FMH. Conversely, if rehearsal were more strongly associated with FMs than encoding factors, or if no special encoding factors were present but the incidence of FMs was high, then the evidence would favour the rehearsal account.

It would appear, then, to be a relatively straightforward matter to choose between the encoding and rehearsal accounts of FM formation: Given an appropriate news item, surprise, consequentiality and rehearsal rates could be measured and the degree of association of these variables with the nature and incidence of FMs could then be assessed. But unfortunately encoding and rehearsal factors cannot be easily separated in this manner. The central problem, as Brown and Kulik observed, is that measures of surprise and consequentiality are often correlated with rate of rehearsal and the reason for this is straightforward: Events which are very surprising and personally significant are usually thought and talked about a great deal. Nevertheless, evaluating the proposal that encoding factors and rehearsal make differential contributions to FM formation remains a possibility, and it is this differential contribution that subsequent studies have focused upon.

Consequentiality and Surprise

Neisser (1982) argued that Brown and Kulik's emphasis on personal consequentiality implied a "great man" theory of history in which the events that befall a prominent leader are felt personally by individuals. Neisser went on to suggest that subjects would have been unlikely to follow Brown and Kulik's personal consequentiality instructions because of this implied "naive" theory of history. It is difficult to know what to make of this criticism, but as we shall see in a later section the negative effect of marginalising Brown and Kulik's emphasis on personal consequentiality has, indeed, had consequences for later studies of FMs. The most notable of these has been a failure on the part of researchers to check that the events assumed to engender FMs were, in fact, personally significant. Failing to check for personal significance renders findings from FM studies ambiguous because it cannot then be known whether an event either should or should not have promoted FM formation.

In addition to this, Neisser pointed out that "consequentiality" is often assigned only *after* an event has been experienced rather than at the time of experience. No doubt consequentiality is influenced by subsequent related events and by reconceptualising an event, but for surprising and personally significant events it could hardly be maintained that no consequentiality is assigned at or close to the time of the experience. Moreover, many events may be assigned preset levels of personal significance that are triggered by the occurrence of an event and fine-tuned by the actual experience and its aftermath—that is, the birth of a child, the death of a relative, the assassination of a leader, even natural disasters such as earthquakes and accidents such as plane crashes, may have preset "personal significance" levels. In short, events may be primed for level of personal consequentiality. Thus, Neisser's claim that consequentiality is often assigned after an event, although undeniably true, overlooks the fact that the personal significance of events is in some sense known before their occurrence and that consequentiality is also assigned at the time of receipt of surprising and personally important news.

Relatedly, Neisser argued that the emphasis on "surprise" by the FMH was also misconceived. The argument here was that high levels of arousal act to narrow the focus of attention and, therefore, are not conducive to the encoding of incidental event details. According to this view, high levels of arousal would not support the "detailed recall of circumstances" (Neisser, 1982, p. 46). Unfortunately, there appears to be little evidence to support this argument; certainly Neisser (1982) does not cite any, and set against it is recent evidence demonstrating that emotional states induced in the laboratory do, in fact, lead to reliably better memory performance than neutral states (Christianson, 1992; Heuer & Reisberg, 1990). It should also be noted that Brown and Kulik may have held something like this view when they proposed that extremely high levels of surprise give rise to retrograde amnesia for a reception event (see Fig. 1.5). In Chapter 4, we will see that Brown and Kulik too may have been incorrect on this point and, on the contrary, extremely high levels of arousal associated with the experience of trauma often lead to intrusive and highly detailed FMs. It seems most probable that both Neisser (1982) and Brown and Kulik (1977) based this aspect of their proposals on the Yerkes–Dodson "law" (Yerkes & Dodson, 1908), which postulates an inverted-"U" shaped function for the relation between arousal and memory where both low and high levels of arousal lead to impaired learning. Recent research indicates that this simple model of arousal and learning is untenable as an account of the relation between memory and emotion (see Christianson, 1992, for a review). Indeed, it now seems that, in general, high levels of emotional arousal lead to detailed and very durable memories.

Content

In keeping with his alternative explanation of the genesis of FMs, that they arise through retelling, Neisser proposed that the content of FMs rather than reflecting "canonical" categories of information in memory actually reflected the operation of "narrative" conventions. In particular, Neisser drew an analogy with newspaper reporters who are instructed to cover the *who, what, where, when* and *why* of the events they report. A good example of this type of narrativisation of a memory account was reported in one of the earliest studies of autobiographical memory by Colegrove (1899). One of Colegrove's subjects recounted the following memory of how he learned the news of the assassination of President Abraham Lincoln some 33 years earlier:

> My father and I were on the road to A- in the state of Main to purchase the "fixings" needed for my graduation. When we were driving down a steep hill into the city we felt that something was wrong. Everybody looked so sad, and there was such terrible excitement that my father stopped his horse, and leaning from the carriage called: "What is it my friends? What has happened?" "Haven't you heard?" was the reply—"Lincoln has been assassinated." The lines fell from my father's limp hands, and with tears streaming from his eyes he sat as one bereft of motion. We were far from home, and much remained to be done, so he rallied after a time and we finished our work as well as our heavy hearts would allow. (Colegrove, 1899, reprinted in Neisser, 1982, p. 41)

Unlike the other reports of FMs we have considered thus far, this account has the feel of a well-rounded tale arising, perhaps from frequent retelling, and would seem to fit well Neisser's rehearsal and narrative conventions account of FMs. In general, it must be the case that an account of a memory is subject to narrative conventions and these will clearly vary with the audience and purpose of the account. But it does not follow that the memory itself arose from narrative conventions. An alternative view is that memories are represented in long-term memory in some particular form and when accessed are only then "edited" into a narrative form for a specific presentation (Anderson & Conway, 1993). The evidence reported by Anderson and Conway (1993) demonstrates that editing a memory takes time and when constraints are placed on the output of information from a memory, such as the requirement for a particular narrative form, then production of memory details is significantly slowed. Thus, the evidence does not support the view that narrative conventions determine directly the structure and content of memories.

One further point on the issue of narrative conventions relates to how these arise. Obviously, there are many different types of conventions constraining and guiding speaker–listener interactions (Grice, 1975), but the convention of reporting events in terms of *who, what, where, when* and *why* would seem to be particularly basic. One possibility is that this convention has arisen because it reflects the structure of memories—in Brown and Kulik's terms, the canonical categories of recall. It would seem to make sense that narrative conventions, where possible, capitalise upon the structure of knowledge in long-term memory; if nothing else, this would reduce the cognitive load, the "editing', in accessing and using long-term memory. Furthermore, from an evolutionary perspective, it might be argued that the emergence of human memory predated the emergence of language and so there was a ready-made opportunity for the nature of memory to influence basic conventions in discourse. Neisser's suggestions concerning the role of narrative conventions in FMs may not then be as problematic for the FMH as previously thought.

Benchmarks

Brown and Kulik proposed that the function of FMs was to provide detailed and durable records of surprising and consequential events. They considered that this might confer a survival advantage in that the rememberer could then re-evaluate the event, share it with others, and prepare future adaptive responses. In contrast, Neisser emphasises the social and cultural functions of FMs, proposing that they are "benchmarks" denoting the intersection of public and private history: "They are the places where we line up our own lives with the course of history itself and say 'I was there' " (Neisser, 1982, p. 48). One shortcoming of the benchmark account is that it is limited to FMs for public events but, as Brown and Kulik found, FMs also exist for personal and private events and these FMs are among the most detailed and consequential of memories. No doubt FMs can act as benchmarks in Neisser's sense of the term but they may also serve other functions. For example, they may more generally serve as personal landmarks in autobiographical memory, they may support the functions suggested by Brown and Kulik, and may fulfil other functions yet to be determined. In short, the benchmark theory seems too limited to account for a wide range of FMs.

Neisser's critique of Brown and Kulik has often been used to discredit what might be termed the "strong encoding" view of FM formation. Upon closer scrutiny, however, it is evident that these criticisms are not decisive for the FMH. The most telling points raised by Neisser relate to the accuracy of FMs and to the role of rehearsal in FM formation, but the evidence offered in support of these points is weak.

THE *CHALLENGER* STUDIES

On 26 January 1986, the space shuttle *Challenger* exploded shortly after take-off, killing all crew. This tragic accident was filmed live and received virtually immediate and protracted coverage in the media. The accident seemed to fit at least part of the specification for an event likely to produce FMs in that it was surprising and newsworthy. Thus, a number of groups of researchers independently initiated FM research programmes for the learning of the news of the *Challenger* disaster. Bohannon (1988) reported a large-scale, between-subjects study in which one group of subjects was sampled within 2 weeks of the event and a second group after an 8-month delay. All subjects completed a three-part FM questionnaire. In the first part of the questionnaire, five questions asked the subjects for: (1) the source of the news (media or another person), (2) an estimate of the number of times they retold the shuttle story, (3) an estimate of the number of times they were exposed to information about the accident (media or another person), (4) an estimate of their emotional reaction on a 5-point rating scale (1 = "couldn't care less" and 5 = "stunned speechless"), and (5) a written account of the reception event including any particularly vivid details. The second part of the questionnaire featured questions that probed specific knowledge of the reception event: (1) day of the week, (2) weather on that day, (3) what were they doing, (4) what were they wearing and (5) where they were. In addition to this, subjects who were informed by another person were also asked (1) what was the name of the other person and (2) what was the other person wearing. The third and final part of the questionnaire assessed memory for facts related to the shuttle mission itself: (1) what time of day did the shuttle explode, (2) what was the date of the accident, (3) what was the name of the shuttle, (4) how long was it into the flight before the explosion, (5) what was the last voice communication between the shuttle and ground control, (6) how many men were on the shuttle and (7) how many women were on the shuttle?

The written accounts of the reception events were scored for the presence of the four categories of *informant, location, ongoing activity* and *time*. Figure 2.1 shows the level of free recall averaged over the four categories for subjects who first learned the news from another person compared with subjects who first learned the news from the media (usually the television). There were significant differences between the "person" and "media" groups in the categories of informant and location where the person group reliably out-performed the media group. These differences

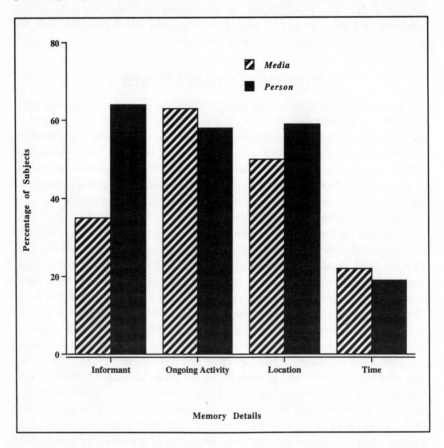

FIG. 2.1. Percentage of subjects recalling information from four canonical categories (data from Bohannon, 1988, table 2).

are interesting and as Bohannon points out appear to reflect a blurring of the "canonical" categories for subjects who learned the news from the media. These subjects could typically recall that they were watching some TV programme that was interrupted by the news but specific details such as who exactly the informant was were less frequently reported by this group. This "TV focus" effect is one which we shall encounter again in later studies and, as already indicated, takes the form of a vivid memory for an interrupted programme without durable retention of other details of the reception event.

The free recall data were also analysed across the two delay periods, 2 weeks and 8 months. In these analyses, only the data from the person group were used and the group was further subdivided on the basis of the ratings from the emotion and rehearsal scales. The subjects who provided a rating of 3 or less on the emotion scale were assigned to a "calm" group and the subjects with higher ratings to an "upset" group. These groups were then further divided and subjects with three or less rehearsals were assigned to a "few" rehearsals group and subjects with more than three rehearsals to a "many" rehearsals group. Figure 2.2 shows the mean free recall scores across these groups. The analyses found a main effect of rehearsal and an interaction between rehearsal and affect. The interaction arose because the "calm–few" group recalled significantly fewer details, at both retention intervals, than any of the other groups who in turn did not differ significantly. The effect of rehearsal, then, is confined to the calm groups and more rehearsals among these subjects lead to the long-term retention of more details. As the upset groups who had low rehearsal rates recalled more details than the corresponding calm groups, then this suggests that emotion too can benefit memory performance.

A similar analysis was performed on the data from the probe questions (the second part of the questionnaire) and the means are shown in Fig. 2.3. In this case, there was a significant main effect of delay and subjects answered more questions at the 2-week than the 8-month retention interval. However, there was also a significant three-way interaction between delay, rehearsal and affect, and the subjects in the "calm–few" 2-week delay group recalled significantly less than the subjects from other groups at this retention interval. In contrast, the subjects in the "many–upset" 8-month delay group recalled reliably more than the subjects from other 8-month delay groups. These findings further suggest that lack of emotional response and rehearsal leads to memories low in event details, whereas more emotion and rehearsal lead to memories with FM characteristics. Finally, the third part of the questionnaire on facts relating to the *Challenger* disaster did not lead to memory performance influenced by emotion and rehearsal. The only effect in these data was that of retention interval, and memory performance was reliably higher at the

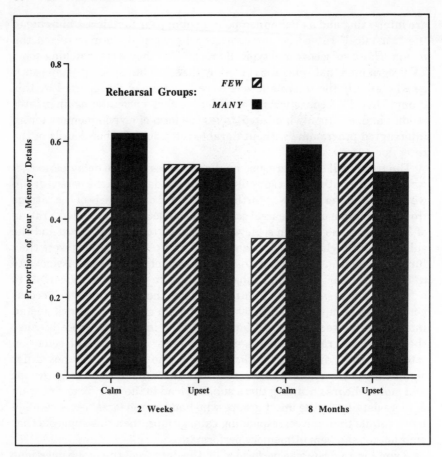

FIG. 2.2. Proportions of memory details for "calm" and "upset" retest groups (data from Bohannon, 1988, table 3).

2-week compared with the 8-month delay. This suggests, interestingly, that the factors which support formation of an autobiographical memory for a reception event do not similarly mediate retention of associated "facts".

Bohannon's (1988) study lends support to both the encoding and rehearsal accounts of FMs and shows that an emotional response coupled with rehearsal produces best memory performance. There are, however, a number of problems with this study that recommend caution in reaching firm conclusions. The most obvious shortcoming is that the personal consequentiality of the *Challenger* disaster was not assessed. Without these data it is impossible to know whether or not this event should have given rise to a high or low incidence of FMs. Bohannon suggests that the emotional rating scale might be thought of as an indicator of personal

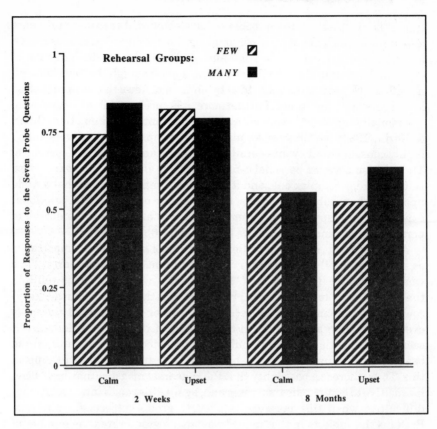

FIG. 2.3. Proportions of responses to probe questions for "calm" and "upset" retest groups (data from Bohannon, 1988, table 4).

consequentiality, but this suggestion is itself open to a number of criticisms. Consider the 5-point scale used in the study, the anchor points of which were 1 = "couldn't care less" and 5 = "stunned speechless". Clearly a score of 1 might be taken as an indicator of personal consequentiality, although how this assesses intensity of emotion is unclear. A score of 5, however, would appear to assess *surprise* rather than personal consequentiality or emotion. There is, then, no straightforward interpretation of this scale, which conflates personal consequentiality and surprise and measures indirectly (if at all) valence and intensity of emotional response. As the scale is open to different and competing interpretations, it is difficult to know what to make of the pattern of findings in which this scale was used to subdivide subjects into groups.

More generally, there is a problematic assumption in this and later studies that emotion and consequentiality are the same thing. But this cannot be the case, as it is possible to have emotional responses to events and stimuli which are of little personal significance (good examples can be found in novels, movies, television and, perhaps, even in the induction of emotional states in the laboratory). Thus, a person might be "shocked and horrified" (Neisser & Harsch, 1992) by an item of news that is nonetheless low in personal importance. Furthermore, it is surely possible to experience a personally significant event without concomitant intense emotion (Rubin & Kozin, 1984; see Chapter 4), although it seems likely that very many highly consequential events entail little significant emotional experience. The relation between personal consequentiality and emotional experience is, therefore, a complex one, and it cannot be simply assumed that a scale upon which a subject indicates the intensity of his or her emotional experience in response to an item of news will also reflect the degree of personal importance of that news (see Chapter 6).

A further issue, discussed by Bohannon and of some critical importance as it relates to all FM studies, is that of the measure of rehearsal. The wording used by Bohannon was "Estimate the number of times you told the shuttle story to others". The problem is that the phrase "shuttle story" could mean a memory for the reception event or a memory for the news event. Bohannon argues that in the context of the FM questionnaire it seems probable that subjects would have provided their estimates on the basis of the first interpretation—but there is no direct evidence to support this. Thus, there is a possibility that the rehearsal measure may have been insensitive to actual rehearsal rates and, again, this raises interpretational difficulties when this measure is used to group subjects for analysis. Perhaps the subjects in the "many" rehearsals group rated the number of rehearsals of both the reception and the news event, whereas subjects in the "few" rehearsals group rated only one of these.

A final problem with Bohannon's study is that these data were not scored in terms of FMs, and it is therefore difficult to make comparisons with Brown and Kulik's study. Recall that Brown and Kulik classed an account as being a FM if the subject answered "Yes" to the question "Do you recall you personal circumstances when you learned … ?" and named at least one canonical category in his or her free recall. In Bohannon's study, the mean number of categories mentioned in free recall was 0.47 with a standard deviation of 0.32, demonstrating that a number of the subjects would not have had FMs if Brown and Kulik's scoring criteria had been employed. The critical question for the FMH relates to degree of association between encoding and rehearsal variables and FMs. But this was not assessed by Bohannon, who only examined the degree of association between encoding and rehearsal variables and recall of *any* type of memory. In summary, Bohannon's study, although reporting intriguing findings, such as dissociation in memory performance dependent upon the source of the news (media or person), is not a critical test of the FMH and this is because of ambiguities in the measures employed and failure to analyse FMs separately.

The aim of McCloskey, Wible, and Cohen's (1988) *Challenger* FM study was to assess directly the strong claims of the FMH. They argued that the FMH implies that FMs are a separate class of memories distinguished by virtue of privileged encoding via a special encoding mechanism that confers upon FMs unique characteristics. According to McCloskey et al. (1988, p. 172), the unique characteristics of FMs are that they are "complete, accurate, vivid, and immune to forgetting". McCloskey et al. used a repeated testing procedure in which a single group of 27 subjects completed a FM questionnaire within 1 week of the *Challenger* disaster and again approximately 9 months later. The subjects answered four critical questions: (1) Where were you when you first learned of the explosion? (2) What were you doing when you first learned of the explosion? (3) Did you see the event at the time it was actually happening, or did you learn about it later? If later, how did you learn about it? (4) What were your first thoughts upon hearing the news? Only examining subjects' abilities to answer these questions at the two delay periods, McCloskey et al. concluded that all their subjects would have had FMs by Brown and Kulik's criteria. However, a comparison of consistencies in responses across the two questionnaires revealed a slightly different picture. Approximately 60.8% of responses to all four questions were classified as totally consistent, a further 25.2% of responses were classified as correct although these were either more specific or more general than the original response, 5.6% of responses were marked as "forgotten", and 8.4% of responses were classified as inconsistent. On the basis of these latter findings, McCloskey et al. concluded that there was no need to postulate a special FM encoding device to account for their findings. Instead, they argued that FMs are like other memories in that they are subject to forgetting and inaccuracies in recall and so are more parsimoniously conceived as the product of general memory processes that feature in the formation of all everyday memories.

McCloskey and co-workers' provocative paper includes many other criticisms of the FMH and has itself been criticised by Schmidt and Bohannon (1988) and by Pillemer (1990), and defended in replies by Cohen, McCloskey, and Wible (1988; 1990). There are, however, two points which make McCloskey and co-workers' interpretation of their findings untenable as a criticism of the FMH. The first is that Brown and Kulik did not argue that FMs were *complete* records of events. In fact, they went to some lengths to make it clear that "completeness" was *not* a distinguishing feature of FMs. Rather, their point was that FMs retained knowledge in an indiscriminate manner. Thus, the position that McCloskey et al. evaluate is a FMH of their own devising and not the FMH proposed by Brown and

Kulik. The second point is that McCloskey et al. took no secondary measures of surprise and personal consequentiality. Indeed, they apparently felt that this was unnecessary and commented that "with regard to surprise and consequentiality, ... the shuttle explosion appears comparable to the events used in previous studies ... Indeed the disaster was widely described in the media as one of those events for which people remember where they were and what they were doing when they learned of it" (McCloskey et al., 1988, p. 172). But such issues cannot be left to opinion and because McCloskey et al. did not assess surprise and consequentiality, their findings are ambiguous. If just a few of their subjects had been unsurprised by the disaster or the event had been of little or no personal consequence to them, then, according to the FMH, these subjects would not have been expected to form FMs. This factor alone can account for the small number of forgotten and inconsistent responses observed in this study. As with many of the single memories discussed earlier, the incompleteness of McCloskey and co-workers' data does not permit a strong test—or, indeed, even a weak test—of the FMH.

Neisser and Harsch (1992) reported their own *Challenger* study in which 106 subjects completed a FM questionnaire within 1 day of the disaster, 32–34 months later 44 of these subjects were retested, and some months after this 40 of the retest subjects were tested yet again in face-to-face interviews. In the FM questionnaire, subjects first provided a free description of how they had learned of the disaster and then answered a series of questions that directly probed the canonical categories. These were questions on time of the reception event, how the news was learned, location, ongoing activity, informant, others present, own feelings, feelings of others, and actions after learning the news. In addition, the subjects also estimated how much time they had spent the previous day in talking about the event and in following coverage in the media. The central purpose of this study was to examine the accuracy of FMs, as Neisser and Harsch assumed that the questionnaire completed within 24 h of the *Challenger* disaster would be basically accurate and responses on the later questionnaire could be used to check how well accuracy was maintained over time. In order to compare the two questionnaires, Neisser and Harsch, in a significant development of research in this area, introduced a novel scoring scheme.

The scoring scheme developed by Neisser and Harsch is important because it is premised on the fact that subjects may be more or less specific in repeatedly describing the same event details and the scheme attempts to quantify this. In order to achieve this, responses on the two questionnaires were compared for each subject on the questions probing location, activity, informant, time and others present. Each attribute was rated on a 3-point scale where 0 indicated a clearly inconsistent answer, 1 a correct answer but one which could be more general or more specific than the original response, and 2 indicated an essentially correct response. In addition to this, Neisser and Harsch defined location, activity and informant as major FM attributes and time of day and others present as minor FM attributes, their reasoning being that errors on any of the major attributes would lead to a memory account that would be strikingly inconsistent, whereas errors on the minor categories, given correct performance on the major attributes, do not lead to radically inconsistent accounts. In order to reflect this in the *weighted attribute scores* (WAS), an extra point was awarded if subjects scored 3 or more on the two minor categories. Thus, the memory scores spanned an 8-point scale of 0–7. A 7 denoted a high degree of agreement between the response to the three major attribute questions (resulting in a score of 6) plus a high degree of consistency on the minor attributes (resulting in a score of 1).

Figure 2.4 shows the percentage of subjects falling at each of the eight points on the WAS scale. It is clear from Fig. 2.4 that very few of these subjects could remember the reception event in which they learned the news of the *Challenger* disaster. Perturbed by these findings, Neisser and Harsch recalled 40 of the retest subjects for face-to-face interviews which attempted to increase the specificity of the cues available for retrieval. In an initial session, they used the "Cognitive Interview" procedure developed by Geiselman, Fisher, MacKinnon, and Holland (1985), which is known to improve witness recall over short retention intervals. The subjects again related their account of the reception event but no effects of the cognitive interview procedures on memory performance were observed. Subjects were then presented with the FM questionnaire they had completed a few months earlier at the 32–34 month retention interval and compared this with the account they had just presented. Most subjects gave the same accounts at these two longer retention intervals and so there were few inconsistencies to resolve. The subjects were then presented with cues based on their original responses 1 day after learning the news, again with no appreciable effect upon accuracy, and finally they were presented with their original FM questionnaire. The subjects who had produced erroneous memories at the 32–34 month retention interval and again a few months later were surprised, if not amazed, by these accounts in their own handwriting which they claimed not to remember.

What form did these errors in recall take? Neisser and Harsch report that although only nine subjects originally claimed to have learned the news from television, at retest this figure had risen to 19, a shift from 21 to 45% of the total sample. A possibility is that the subjects were making "wrong time slice" errors. Many, if not all, of Neisser and Harsch's subjects would have watched the repeated television coverage of the accident *after* the original reception event in which they first learned the news. The TV priority evident at the 32–34 month retention interval may have occurred

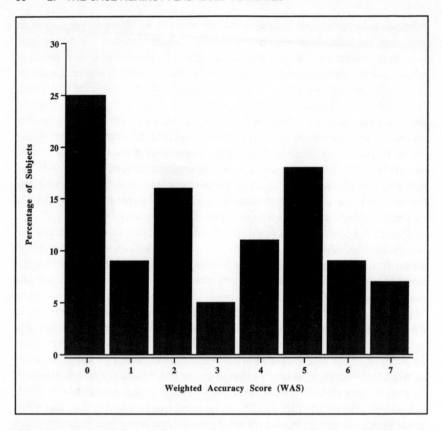

FIG. 2.4. Percentage of subjects' weighted accuracy scores (WAS) (after Neisser & Harsch, 1992, fig. 2.1).

because the subjects recalled watching the televised news of the disaster rather than the original reception event. Indeed, it seems highly probable that when an item of news is presented in a number of different reception contexts and there is nothing to distinguish one context from another, then different memories will be recalled on different occasions. Thus, many of the errors noted by Neisser and Harsch would seem to fit the "wrong time slice" explanation, although for a few of the inconsistent memories this explanation appears less appropriate. For example, one subject originally reported learning the news while eating her lunch in a cafeteria. At retest this same subject recalled a girl running down her hall on campus screaming and she then turned on her television and watched the news coverage of the disaster. Neisser and Harsch speculate that this type of error may reflect a failure of source monitoring at encoding, as discussed earlier in connection with Johnson's (1985) memory. The subject may have wanted to express her response to the news by running and screaming, and it is possible this was fantasised and became incorporated in her memory to be reproduced later in a plausible form.

Despite the innovation in scoring FM questionnaire responses and the fascinating account of error responses, Neisser and Harsch's study suffers from the same faults as other studies of the *Challenger* disaster. Most crucially the personal consequentiality of the event was not assessed and, therefore, it cannot be known whether or not the subjects *should* have had FMs. A further problem relates to actual collection of FM information. It is not clear from Neisser and Harsch's description of their study that the subjects had the opportunity to respond "don't know" or "forgotten" to the various items on the retest questionnaire and direct questions in the interview. Neisser and Harsch report that only two of their subjects declined the questionnaire claiming that they could not remember, but the key issue is whether or not each item in the questionnaire was accompanied by an option which allowed the subject to indicate forgetting. The implicit task demands of the questionnaire may have lead subjects to make responses which they believed *must* have been true of the reception event but which, nonetheless, were not actually remembered. By way of illustrating this point, my own memory of learning of the shuttle disaster consists of a highly vivid image of the *Challenger* accelerating at enormous speed at an angle against the backdrop of a blue sky when suddenly a plume of white gas briefly billowed out from the side of the craft and in the next instant it exploded. I can still hear the sound of the voices of the crew and ground control, although I can distinguish no words. I would certainly rate this as a highly vivid image and would infer from it that I *must* have been watching TV when I learned the news. A few further inferences on my general personal circumstances in 1986 would allow me to construct detailed and plausible responses to a FM questionnaire such as that used by Neisser and Harsch. The key point, however, is that I would not have *remembered* my personal circumstances. Perhaps this is what occurred for some of the subjects in Neisser and Harsch's study. Responding to the implicit demand of the retest questionnaire *that they should remember this event*, the subjects may have reconstructed a plausible memory, of which possibly they were unaware that they were constructing, and it was a memory of this reconstruction that was recalled some weeks later when the subjects were tested for a third time. In short, because no FMs were formed at encoding, possibly because the *Challenger* disaster although surprising did not generate sufficiently high levels of personal importance, then memories were later inferred in response to implicit demands of the retest FM questionnaire.

Neisser and Harsch also collected measures of rehearsal and emotional response. Curiously, the measure of rehearsal only referred to exposure to the *Challenger* event and reception event *on the day* of the disaster. This is odd, as rehearsal is central to Neisser's (1982) view of FM formation and as he pointed out unfolds over a period of days, weeks and years. If this view is accepted, then it is hardly surprising that Neisser and Harsch's measure of rehearsal failed to correlate with consistency in the memory reports—quite simply, it was not a sensitive measure of rehearsal, which is a process that unfolds over time. The measure of emotion was similarly questionable in that subjects were asked "How did you feel about it?" and Neisser and Harsch constructed a quantitative scale on the basis of the subjects' comments, which also, but not surprisingly, failed to correlate with memory consistency. Such a measure is far from satisfactory, as subjects are not asked directly to indicate the nature and intensity of their emotions. In summary, Neisser and Harsch's study provides interesting data on memory reconstruction, but it is not clear how these data bear on the FMH.

STUDIES OF OTHER PUBLIC EVENTS: AN ASSASSINATION, A WAR AND A PUBLIC DISASTER

One of the FM studies that comes closest to investigating the type of event that Brown and Kulik singled out as most likely to produce FMs was conducted by Christianson (1989). In this investigation, a group of 36 Swedish subjects took part in a test–retest study for the assassination of the Swedish Prime Minister Olof Palme. The subjects completed a FM memory questionnaire, similar to those described above, 6 weeks after the assassination and again 52–54 weeks later. In addition to providing memory details, the subjects also rated how "upsetting" and surprising they had found the news. Most subjects reported a negative emotional reaction to the news and all subjects were extremely surprised. On a "lenient" scoring criteria (i.e. a subject's response was "basically" rather than "exactly" correct), it was found that over 90% of Christianson's subjects had FM memories. However, using a stricter scoring criteria which required the subjects to be *exactly* correct in their retest responses, the incidence of FM memories fell to just over 50%. In further analyses, it was found that the secondary variables of emotion and surprise were not generally related to the incidence of FM memories with the exception that on the lenient scoring criteria, the subjects who were most surprised were reliably more consistent in their memory reports than the subjects who were somewhat less surprised. This, then, would appear to be good evidence that FMs are not automatically formed in response to surprising and emotional news events.

However, and yet again, a problem with Christianson's study was that subjects did not judge the consequentiality or importance of the event and so it is not known whether or not this crucial factor influenced memory formation. For instance, a person may have been "shocked and surprised" by the news of Palme's murder, but the event may nonetheless have been of little personal consequence. If this was the case for Christianson's subjects, then FM memory formation would have been attenuated. A further and equally pressing problem relates to the sensitivity of the measures of intensity of emotion and surprise. Recall that Christianson's subjects were only first questioned 6 weeks after learning of the news and the sensitivity of these measures therefore crucially depends upon the subjects recalling accurately the *degree* to which they were upset and surprised. If the subjects could not do this, then their judgements would not be accurate and would be unlikely to be related to memory consistency. In connection with this, Pillemer (1984; see Chapter 3) found that ratings of affect and surprise taken 6 months after a FM memory event were unrelated to memory consistency and this strongly suggests that such measures must be taken reasonably close to the event. In Pillemer's study, ratings taken within 1 month proved to be reliably associated with memory consistency. The 6-week delay in the Christianson study may, then, have been associated with a lowering of the effectiveness of these rating scales. In summary, Christianson's study suffers from some of the flaws noted in the *Challenger* series and, therefore, cannot be taken as critical evidence against the FMH.

Weaver (1993) conducted a FM study in which subjects recalled a personal memory of meeting a friend in the preceding 7 days. Fortuitously, at the time of Weaver's study, President Bush announced the start of the bombing of Iraq and Weaver was able to incorporate this into his study by asking subjects to recall also the reception event in which they learned this news. Thus, Weaver was able to compare directly memory for an everyday event with memory for a news event that might have been expected to lead to FMs. Weaver's subjects were retested twice, at delays of 3 months and 1 year, and in the original test and two retests completed a questionnaire similar to that employed by Christianson. Crucially, Weaver also collected ratings of surprise, consequentiality and emotion—but only for the reception event and not for the everyday event. Weaver's main findings were that there were few differences in the retention of event details for the two types of event, both events showed forgetting over the first 3 months of retention, and memories then stabilised and there was little forgetting between the retests at 3 months and 1 year. The subjects' responses to items on the original and retest FM questionnaires, which as usual sampled event details such as location, time of day, activity, and so on, were scored for consistency on a "lenient" criteria (i.e. they were basically but not exactly the same across questionnaires) and a "strict" criteria (i.e. exactly the same across questionnaires). The subjects remembered few specific details and the mean number of subjects remembering information from all the categories on the strict scoring criteria was approximately 30% for the personal event and 20% for the reception event. Memory scored on the lenient scale was, however, considerably better with means of approximately 71% and 63%, respectively. This aspect of the findings indicates that the majority of subjects had general rather than specific memories for both the personal and reception events.

The key question for the FMH is whether or not the news of the bombing of Iraq was associated with high levels of surprise, personal consequentiality and emotion. Strangely, Weaver neither reported the exact scales used to assess these critical encoding factors or any of the data resulting from them and, moreover, the ratings do not feature in any of the analyses. Thus, it is not possible to judge whether or not this news item should have lead to the widespread formation of FMs and, consequently, it is difficult to know what to conclude from Weaver's study. Certainly, the finding of no differences in recall between the private and public memories cannot be used to sustain Weaver's argument that no special encoding mechanism is required for FM formation, and this is because no evidence is presented to show that conditions appropriate to FM formation (high consequentiality, emotion and surprise) prevailed in the first place.

Wright (1993) used a cross-sectional design in a FM study for learning news of the "Hillsborough" disaster which occurred during an important football match between Liverpool and Nottingham Forest when 95 people were crushed to death. The event was immediately and widely reported in the UK and separate groups of subjects in Wright's study completed a FM questionnaire 2 days, 1 month and 5 months after the event. As the same subjects were not retested the consistency, and hence accuracy, of memory reports could not be assessed in this study. Nevertheless, Wright found no reliable differences between the groups at the different retention intervals, all of whom were able to recall information on at least one of the canonical categories. However, the most intriguing aspect of Wright's findings was that ratings of personal and societal importance increased over time and, even more tantalising, the correlation between personal importance and emotion also increased from 0.48 to 0.70. Wright's interpretation of these findings is that as retention interval increases, so a memory is gradually recoded into a stable representation in long-term memory in which importance and emotion become closely associated. Possibly, this might indicate some slow process of consolidation acting over months rather than over minutes and hours. Whatever the case, the findings imply that memories are not simply formed by some type of "special" encoding device operating during or shortly after the reception event. Unfortunately, these findings are open to other interpretations. For instance, because different groups of subjects were tested at different retention intervals, the differences in mean importance and emotion ratings may simply reflect group differences rather than changes on these scales over time. Furthermore, mean importance ratings never rose above the mid-point on the importance rating scale, indicating that for most subjects in Wright's study the Hillsborough disaster was not a personally important event. For this reason alone, these data do not bear directly on the FMH; instead, they suggest that the Hillsborough disaster was unlikely to give rise to the widespread formation of FMs.

CONCLUSIONS

Perhaps the most remarkable feature of these studies, which have been so critical of the notion of FMs and the FMH, is their almost complete failure to include measures to assess whether FMs either should or should not have been formed. Given the very strong emphasis in Brown and Kulik's original FM paper on the critical role of personal consequentiality, this seems a remarkable omission. There are, however, a number of obvious reasons why researchers omitted to check for personal consequentiality. One reason is that, unlike Brown and Kulik's study, the studies described in this chapter did not compare the incidence of FMs across different groups of subjects and, therefore, it was possible to assume rather than measure personal consequentiality. A strong clue that this did in fact occur is present in the earlier quote from McCloskey et al. (1988, p. 172), in which the authors comment on the *Challenger* explosion: "the disaster was widely described in the media as one of those events for which people remember where they were and what they were doing when they learned of it". The fact that many people *believed* that an event was a flashbulb event may have lured researchers into assuming high personal consequentiality rather then checking that this was, in reality, the case. Another reason for ignoring personal consequentiality may have stemmed from Neisser's (1982) claim that personal consequentiality implied a "naive" theory of history to which subjects would be unlikely to subscribe. If this argument is accepted (and I suggested above that it should not be), then it is unlikely that one would include such a provocative measure in one's FM study. Whatever the reason, the fact is that because measures of personal consequentiality were either not taken, or when taken not reported, in the studies reviewed in this chapter (with the exception of Wright, 1993), no decision can be made as to what the incidence of FMs *should* have been according to Brown and Kulik's theory. Thus, the findings from these studies do not directly engage the FMH.

Evidence for Flashbulb Memories

Almost since its inception, the FMH and the concept of FMs has been under concerted attack. The previous chapter showed that purely theoretical criticisms and single instances of memories do not provide convincing evidence against the FMH. Similarly, many of the studies that have concluded against the FMH can themselves be shown to contain flaws that weaken their credibility and, in some instances, their findings are subject to multiple interpretations. The studies of FMs to be considered in the present chapter are less open to such criticisms and, generally, have tended to provide evidence of FMs. This evidence, however, by no means gives overwhelming or uncritical support to the FMH, which still appears to require revision in several respects. Nevertheless, there is evidence for the existence of FMs and it is to this that we now turn.

THE ATTEMPTED ASSASSINATION OF RONALD REAGAN

Pillemer (1984) conducted a FM study for memories associated with the attempted assassination of President Ronald Reagan that took place on 30 March 1981. In Pillemer's study, a group of 83 subjects were tested 1 month after the assassination attempt, of whom 44 were retested 5½ months later, i.e. 6½ months after the assassination attempt (referred to hereafter as the 7-month group). In addition, a further group of 38 subjects were tested once only at the the 7-month retention interval. Thus, there were three groups of subjects: two independent groups, one tested at the 1-month delay and the other at the 7-month delay, and the retest group originally tested at the 1-month delay and tested again at the 7-month delay. The subjects completed a FM questionnaire which first asked them "Do you recall the circumstances in which you first heard the news of this event?" The subjects who answered "Yes" to this question then wrote a free description of their memory of the reception event. In the second section of the questionnaire, the subjects answered direct questions on the six canonical categories employed by Brown and Kulik (1977) and described any images which came to mind when they remembered the event, any thoughts they had on learning the news, and the number of times they had rehearsed the memory. Finally, in the third part of the questionnaire, subjects rated the following on 5-point scales: (a) the intensity of their emotional reaction when first learning the news, (b) degree of surprise when first learning the news, (c) degree of "impact" of the news, (d) degree of impact in retrospect, (e) perceived severity of injury when first learning the news, (f) present opinion of Reagan, (g) opinion of Reagan prior to the shooting and (h) type of emotion experienced. All the subjects completed the questionnaire and the retest group completed it twice, once at the 1-month delay and once at the 7-month delay.

The subjects were scored as having a FM if they answered "Yes" to the question "Do you recall the circumstances in which you first heard the news of this event?" and gave a memory description. (Note that this approximates to the "lenient" classification of FMs used in some of the studies described in Chapter 2.) Using these criteria, a high incidence of FMs was found and Fig. 3.1 shows the mean percentages of FMs by groups. It can be seen from Fig. 3.1 that over the whole sample approximately 92% of the subjects had FMs, an incidence comparable with the FM rate observed by Brown and Kulik for events such as the assassinations of JFK and Martin Luther King. In order to further analyse these data, Pillemer counted how many of Brown and Kulik's six canonical categories were mentioned in each free recall protocol. Figure 3.2 shows the mean number of canonical categories for each group. Although there were no reliable differences between the independent groups at the two delay periods, there was a significant decrease in the number of canonical categories mentioned by the retest groups and the 1-month group recalled more than the 7-month group. This might reflect forgetting or it might reflect, as Pillemer suggests, some consolidation of a FM over time. There is, however, an important point here and that is that the subjects were not required to mention *any* canonical categories in their free recall memory accounts. Consequently, the direct questions that probed memory for each category individually are a better measure of the retention. Pillemer found that his subjects were able to respond to all six canonical categories when directly questioned and

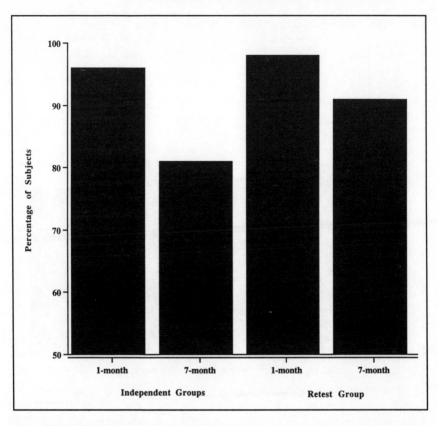

FIG. 3.1. Percentage of subjects with flashbulb memories in independent and retest groups (data from Pillemer, 1984).

performance across all groups was in excess of 90%. But this impressive level of performance should be treated with caution, as many responses were short and unspecific and could, perhaps, have been inferences rather than recollections. One further finding relating to FMs was that approximately 71% of the subjects reported and described visual images featuring in their recall compared with an average of only 25% for non-visual sensory memories. Taken together, these findings constitute impressive evidence of a high incidence of durable and vivid recollections of learning the news of the attempted assassination of Ronald Reagan. By way of illustration of the high level of details in these FMs, Pillemer provides the following example:

On the afternoon it occurred, my husband and I were returning from a holiday in the Caribbean and had reached the Miami Airport. We were

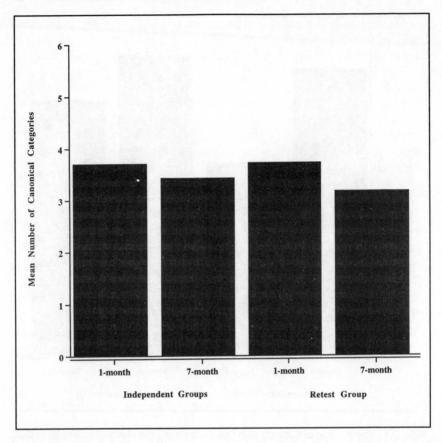

FIG. 3.2. Mean number of canonical categories for independent and retest groups (data from Pillemer, 1984, table 2).

standing in line to check baggage or tickets or something, with other people near and people passing to and fro. I heard a man next to me say to his companion "You heard about the President," and the other one say something like "Yes, have they got the guy who shot him?" I cannot recall the exact wording but I know that I had learned someone had shot President Reagan and some news about it already existed. My immediate reaction was "Oh God, here we go again," and then a feeling of resignation, depression, we have been through this before and it was terrible, and an ironic recall of the superstition that Presidents elected in years 00, 20, 60, 80, etc. will not finish their terms alive. We boarded the plane before we heard any more, and then I was asked by a young couple, visibly shaken if I knew anything. Shortly after the plane took off the captain made an announcement giving all the information he had up to that time. (Pillemer, 1984, p. 64)

Given that here we actually have strong evidence for a high incidence of FMs, the critical issues for the FMH relate to memory consistency and predictors of the elaborateness of memories. In dealing with these issues, we will focus on Pillemer's analyses of the retest groups but first consider the data from the 5-point rating scales for rehearsal, emotion, surprise and impact. In the independent groups, 76% of subjects gave ratings of 1, indicating that they had not overtly recounted their memories. All the members of the retest group had recounted their memory at least once on the original memory questionnaire, but for 56% of these subjects this had been the only occasion of retelling the memory. For all groups, slightly above moderate levels of emotion and surprise were experienced (mean values = 3.16 and 3.44, respectively). However, the "impact" of the event upon subjects was judged to be low at the time of the reception event (mean = 2.24), and to be of little or no impact in retrospect (mean = 1.81). These findings suggest that because the news led to low rehearsal rates and was of low impact, then these factors are unlikely to play any prominent role in the formation and maintenance of FMs to the attempted assassination of Ronald Reagan. In contrast, it seems probable that the moderate to high levels of emotion and surprise may be associated with memory elaborateness and durability.

In order to investigate the effects of rehearsal, emotion and surprise, the consistency of responses to the direct questions probing the six canonical categories at the 1-month and 7-month delays were computed. Responses were coded as consistent/inconsistent according to whether they were in general agreement, for example, "working at my desk" (1-month response) and "grading papers at my desk" (7-month response) were coded as consistent. Using this procedure it was found that responses were highly consistent over the retention interval and on a scale of 0 (no response to any of the six questions consistent) to 6 (responses to all six questions consistent) the overall mean consistency score was 4.88. As Pillemer comments, the subjects generally knew who they were with, where they were, what they were doing and how they felt when they learned the news of the attempted assassination. Correlations between the ratings of rehearsal, emotion and surprise from the 1-month questionnaire and the 7-month questionnaire and memory consistency score were then computed. Significant positive correlations between 1-month emotion ratings and consistency score ($r=0.28$) and between 1-month surprise ratings and consistency ($r=0.28$) were found. There were no significant correlations between any of the other measures at either the 1-month or 7-month delays and consistency scores. Thus, rehearsal was not found to be associated with FMs.

The retest group also supplied descriptions of their memory imagery in the 1-month and 7-month questionnaires and a comparison of consistency of imagery was, therefore, possible. Twenty-three of the subjects retested described images on both questionnaires and of these 19 were judged as consistent. The ratings of these subjects were then compared with the ratings of subjects who were inconsistent or who did not recall images. For the retest subjects with consistent images, both emotion and surprise ratings from the 1-month questionnaire predicted consistency. Also in this analysis 1-month ratings of impact approached significance. Ratings from the 7-month questionnaire were not reliably associated with image consistency, nor were rehearsal ratings from either questionnaire. This then is further evidence that the more emotional, surprising and impactful an item of news, the more likely the formation of memories that feature durable and vivid visual imagery.

Finally, Pillemer reports one further intriguing aspect of the data. Many of the subjects (over 62%) from all the groups reported thinking of related news events during the reception event. This often took the form of remembering other assassinations or assassination attempts, especially that of JFK, or of contemporary political events. These remindings (Schank, 1982) are particularly interesting, suggesting as they do some rapid integration of the reception event with knowledge structures in long-term memory. Indeed, further analyses found that approximately 25% of subjects reported explicitly recalling their personal circumstances when learning of other assassinations and attempted assassinations during the reception event for the attempted assassination of Reagan. As the item on the questionnaire did not request this information directly, it seems clear that this must be an underestimation of such remindings, which would have undoubtedly occurred in more than a quarter of the subjects.

Although Pillemer takes his findings as generally supporting the FMH, he postulates that for the FM system to function effectively there must also be some special retrieval mechanism, which he calls a *flashback* mechanism. Pillemer proposes that when an emotional and surprising event occurs, this induces a particular but general affective state in an individual and this state serves to activate in long-term memory associated memories of events in which similar affect was experienced. The evidence from subjects' accounts of how they were reminded of related public events when learning of the attempted assassination of Ronald Reagan clearly supports this proposal. Furthermore, a general activation of affect-associated memories may support the rapid integration of a current reception event with other knowledge already represented in long-term memory and in this way facilitate the creation of a stable and durable memory.

Pillemer's study provides strong evidence of FMs but does not support one central conjecture of the FMH, namely that personal consequentiality is a critical factor in FM formation. The measure of personal consequentiality employed by Pillemer was a rating of the "impact" of the news on a person's life. But from the account provided in Pillemer (1984) it is not clear that this corresponds to Brown and Kulik's carefully worded questions on personal consequentiality. If anything, the use of the term "impact" suggests both national and personal significance. Nevertheless, it seems clear that the attempted assassination, at least in retrospect, did not have wide-ranging personal or national consequences. Rehearsal, too, was not found to be associated with FMs and the subjects in this study basically did not recount their memory of the reception event to others. Yet FMs were formed and formation was only associated with intensity of affect and degree of surprise experienced during the reception event. This suggests that both the FMH and competitor theories, such as rehearsal theory, may require revision.

THE SAN FRANCISCO EARTHQUAKE

One of the most interesting of recent FM studies was reported in a conference paper by Neisser, Winograd, and Weldon (1991). In this study, 36 subjects from Berkeley and 44 from Santa Cruz who had direct experience of the 1989 California earthquake completed the Neisser and Harsch (1992) FM questionnaire for their personal circumstances when first learning of (experiencing) the earthquake and for their personal circumstances when learning of the collapse of the Bay Bridge (which had not been experienced directly but which was associated with the quake). In addition, a further 76 subjects from Emory campus in Atlanta who had no direct experience of the earthquake also completed the FM questionnaire. All the subjects completed their first questionnaire close to the time of the events, although for logistical reasons this varied across sites, and then completed a second questionnaire approximately 18 months later. For each of these groups, weighted accuracy scores (WASs) were calculated in a manner similar to that described by Neisser and Harsch, although some slight modifications were made in the types of canonical categories sampled. Figure 3.3 shows the mean WASs for all these retest groups and for the 44 subjects in Neisser and Harsch's *Challenger* study.

The left-hand columns in Fig. 3.3 show that subjects who had direct experience of the earthquake had remarkably detailed memories 18 months after the event. Weighted accuracy scores averaging higher than 6 meant that the subjects remembered all the details probed in the original questionnaire and were slightly more general about only one of these details at retest. Direct experience, then, would seem to promote the formation of FMs. However, the middle columns in Fig. 3.3 show that the subjects who experienced the earthquake also had highly detailed

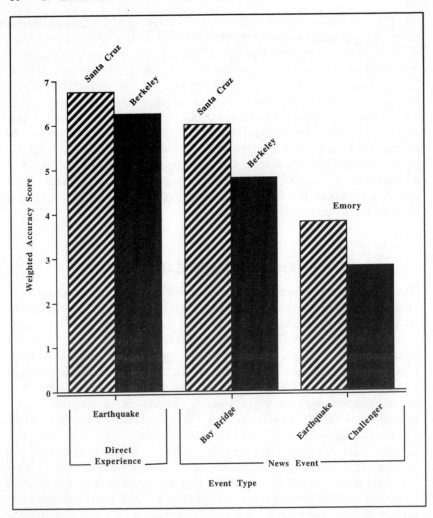

FIG. 3.3. Mean weighted accuracy scores for direct experience and news event groups (after Neisser et al., 1991).

memories for learning of the collapse of the Bay Bridge. With a mean WAS across the two groups close to 6, it is clear that there was a high incidence of FMs for this news event among those individuals who actually experienced the earthquake. For the subjects from Emory who did not have direct experience of the earthquake, WAS scores were significantly lower and averaged about 4, indicating reasonably detailed memories but ones which were, perhaps, more similar to the *Challenger* memories than to the FMs of the direct experience groups.

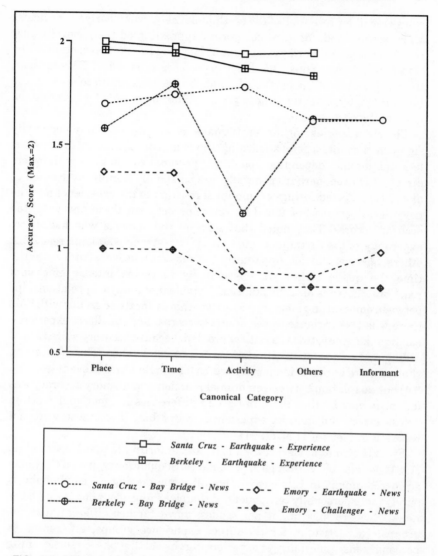

FIG. 3.4. Mean accuracy scores on five memory attributes for direct experience and news event groups (after Neisser et al., 1991).

Figure 3.3 shows the WASs decomposed into accuracy scores for each of the canonical categories (note that the category "informant" does not apply to the direct experience groups). This more detailed analysis reveals the same basic pattern, with the direct experience groups having virtually perfect recall for all categories and good recall for most categories relating to reception of the Bay Bridge news This contrasts with the Emory group, whose recall for reception of the earthquake news was clearly worse across all categories and, for some categories, approximated the generally poor recall observed earlier by Neisser and Harsch (1992) for reception of the *Challenger* news. Thus, the direct experience groups had FMs for both their experience of the earthquake and for learning of the collapse of the Bay Bridge, whereas the Emory group did not have FMs for learning the news of the earthquake.

Clearly, experiencing an earthquake is an unusual and personally significant event, whereas learning about an earthquake in the news is less unique and, depending upon one's personal connections with others directly involved, perhaps generally less personally significant. Neisser et al. (1991) collected ratings of emotional reaction to the experience and the news in all groups but found no relations between these and weighted accuracy scores. They noted that some of the subjects who had direct experience of the earthquake did indeed have strong emotional reactions; others, however, did not. Apparently, the subjects who were outdoors at the time the quake struck were less likely to report intense emotional reactions. There is also the additional problem of analysing relationships between emotion and memory accuracy—that is, for those groups with FMs there was less variance in the accuracy scores. For the direct experience earthquake group, this is a critical problem because accuracy scores are at ceiling and so no statistical relations can be established. The same group showed more variance in memory scores for the Bay Bridge event (see Fig. 3.4) but no relation between emotional reaction and memory accuracy was found. It may be that there are group differences in emotional reaction across direct and indirect experience groups but, if so, these were not reported by Neisser et al. (1991).

From the point of view of the FMH, it is unfortunate that Neisser et al. (1991) did not collect ratings of personal consequentiality, even if they may seem redundant in this case—after all, experiencing an earthquake is surely more personally consequential than learning about one through the news. Such ratings might nonetheless have further differentiated the groups. In particular, for the direct experience groups, differences in personal consequentiality to experiencing the earthquake versus learning about the collapse of the Bay Bridge might have been especially revealing. Following the reasoning of the FMH, it would be expected that slight but consistent changes in personal consequentiality would lead to variations in the elaborateness of FMs, such that lower personal consequentiality for reception of the Bay Bridge news would be associated with less elaborate FMs. This appears to be exactly what Neisser et al. (1991) found, as shown in Figs 3.3 and 3.4. No doubt a more detailed report of this study would shed further light on factors associated with the high incidence of FMs in the direct experience groups.

THE RESIGNATION OF MARGARET THATCHER

Conway et al. (1994) conducted a large-scale, cross-national, test–retest FM study for the resignation of British Prime Minister, Margaret Thatcher. In this study, a large group of subjects completed a FM questionnaire within 14 days of her resignation, a subset of whom were retested approximately 11 months later, and at the same point a new group completed the FM questionnaire for the first time. Approximately two-thirds of all subjects were UK nationals and the remaining one-third were drawn from other nationalities (mainly North American). Table 3.1 shows the distribution of subjects by nationality. The purpose of the study was to test directly the FMH by investigating the incidence and nature of FMs in populations who might reasonably be expected to differ in frequency of FMs for the resignation. In the UK, the resignation of Mrs Thatcher was surprising and significant. It marked the end of a political era during which fundamental changes had taken place in British society, most of which stemmed directly from the policies and actions of the Thatcher governments. Moreover, the 11 years that the Thatcher governments were in office corresponds to a period during which many of the subjects would have first become politically aware (cf. Schuman & Rieger, 1992). Indeed, it would be fair to say that UK citizens aged 18–25 years at the time of the resignation had virtually no direct experience of any other government. Obviously this was not the case for the non-UK group, who although aware of the political status of Prime Minister Thatcher would not have been influenced so strongly.

On the day of the resignation and the day following, we ran a small pilot study using the FM questionnaire described by Pillemer (1984). The initial findings indicated that various modifications were needed to the FM questionnaire if it were to be applicable to our subject sample and a number of changes were introduced. As with previous questionnaires, subjects first answered "Yes" or "No" to the question "Do you recall your personal

TABLE 3.1
Distribution of Subjects by Conditions (from Conway et al., 1994)

	Test	Retest	New	Totals
UK	613	215	709	1537
Non-UK	310	154	316	780
Totals	923	369	1025	2317

circumstances when first learning the news of the resignation of Margaret Thatcher?" They then wrote a short description of the reception event and answered a series of direct questions which asked who they were with, where they were, what they were doing and what had been the source of the news (person or media). The subjects then completed a series of 3-point rating scales for surprise, intensity of affect, knowledge of the Thatcher governments and interest in politics. In addition, the subjects also indicated whether the news had reminded them of any related events and, if so, they were asked to describe these. The major change to the questionnaire was to represent consequentiality by two rating scales: one required a judgement of how *personally important* the news was and the other required a judgement of its *national importance*. In the pilot study, subjects had experienced difficulty in separating personal and national importance when responding to the consequentiality question, and presenting these as two distinct questions solved this problem (see also Rubin & Kozin, 1984, discussed in Chapter 4). Finally, the subjects rated on three separate scales how often they had thought about the event, spoken about it, and listened/watched/read coverage in the media.

Responses to the questionnaires were scored as follows. For the subjects tested only within 14 days of the news (the "original" group) and for the subjects tested only at the 11-month retention interval (the "new" group), scores of 1 were awarded for providing a memory description, and for answering the probe questions on people, place, activity and source of the news. A total score of 5 was classified as a FM. In scoring the retest group, the scoring method developed by Neisser and Harsch (1992) was employed and for each of the five memory attributes subjects were awarded a score between 0 and 2 according to consistency of answers across the two tests. A score of 0 indicated a forgotten or wholly inconsistent response, 1 indicated a response that was generally but not exactly consistent, and 2 indicated an exactly consistent response. The five memory attributes were not weighted and all contributed equally to a total FM score ranging between 0 and 10. For convenience, these scores were proportionalised to range from 0 to 1 and scores of 0.9 and 1 were classified as FMs.

Figure 3.5 shows the percentages of subjects classified as having FMs. These percentages are presented simply to provide a rough indication of how detailed memories were across the groups and it should be noted that: (1) the "original" group may not have had FMs, as the crucial factor of consistency over time does not contribute to scoring these memories, and (2) the scoring of the retest group differed from that of the other groups. Nevertheless, Fig. 3.5 indicates that actually completing the FM questionnaire apparently had little effect on the UK retest group because the subjects in the "new" UK group, who completed the FM questionnaire only once, showed a comparable frequency of FMs. There is, however, an

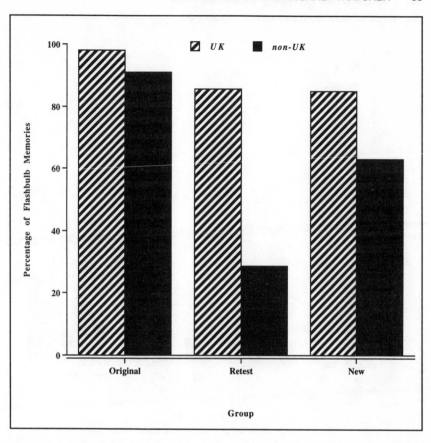

FIG. 3.5. Percentage of flashbulb memories for original, retest and new groups (after Conway et al., 1994).

interesting discrepancy between the retest non-UK group and the "new" non-UK group, with the latter showing a higher incidence of FMs than the former. The consistency of responses in the "new" non-UK group could not be checked but, as we shall see, it seems possible that at least some of the responses that contributed to this overall score may have originated from erroneous memories.

The striking finding depicted in Fig. 3.6 is that the UK retest group had a far higher incidence of FMs than the non-UK group. Figure 3.6 shows the distribution of memory consistency scores for the UK and non-UK groups and it can be seen that for the UK group most memories were classified as highly consistent (scores in the 0.9 and 1 categories). For the non-UK group, however, most memories were classified as inconsistent or forgotten. These differences in FM frequency across the two national groups parallel those

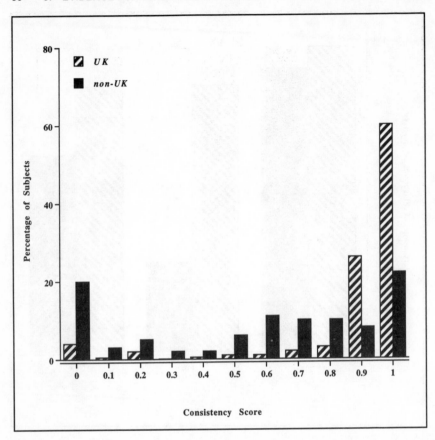

FIG. 3.6. Percentage of subjects' memory scores for the UK and non-UK groups (after Conway et al., 1994, fig. 1).

observed earlier by Brown and Kulik for groups of Black and White Americans and clearly reflect variability in the consequentiality, importance and impact of the resignation.

The cross-national differences demonstrate that the incidence of FMs varied across different sub-groups. More important from the point of view of the FMH are differences between subjects with and without FMs, and Fig. 3.7 shows the mean consistency scores for each of the five memory attributes (description, people, activity, place and source) for the FM and non-FM groups. The subjects with FMs were almost completely correct on all memory attributes, with only the scores for description differing reliably from each of the other scores. This was because the subjects tended to be slightly more general and brief in their retest memory descriptions. For the non-FM group, description differed reliably from people and activity,

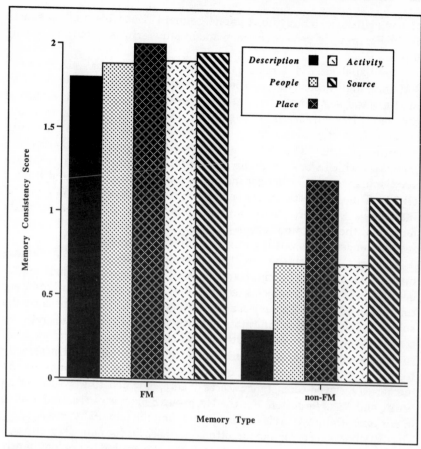

FIG. 3.7. Mean memory attribute accuracy scores for FM and non-FM groups (from Conway et al., 1994, fig. 2).

people differed reliably from place and source, but neither people and activity nor place and source differed reliably. Thus, Fig. 3.7 shows that in the non-FM group, memory for the reception event of learning of Margaret Thatcher's resignation fragmented over time. The ability to provide a coherent memory description declined markedly, as did memory for other people and activity. Memory for location and source of the news (other person or media) was more durable, but even in these cases the mean consistency scores of slightly higher than 1 indicated that this knowledge was not highly specific or exact. For example, a subject at retest might remember that she had originally been at home watching the television when she learned of the resignation, which contrasts with the high degree of specificity of her original response, which might have been "at home in the living room watching the news on Channel 4". Such "general" responses in the FM group were very common and by our scoring scheme gained only 1 point.

These analyses of the memory attribute data show that subjects with FMs gave highly consistent and detailed memory descriptions over a period of 11 months, suggesting that this group have highly specific and enduring memories. In contrast, the subjects who did not have FM memories gave incomplete and inconsistent memory descriptions over the 11-month retention interval. The data suggest that this group had fragmentary memories which were not highly detailed and specific—indeed, they are very similar to the *Challenger* memories collected by Neisser and Harsch (1992). Thus, subjects in the non-FM group showed all the signs of individuals who were in the process of forgetting or who had already forgotten the reception event in which they learned of Thatcher's resignation, and this was the case regardless of nationality.

In order to study the nature of error response more closely, a count was made of the non-FMs (memories with consistency scores less than 0.9) for both UK and non-UK subjects (see Fig. 3.6). In this count, non-FMs were counted as *forgotten* if a subject's consistency score had arisen because the subject failed to provide information on any or all of the questions relating to the five memory attributes. Other non-FMs were classed as *errors* when the consistency scores had arisen because the subject responded incorrectly to any or all of the attribute questions. For the non-UK subjects, 31 memories received consistency scores of zero, of which 15 were classed as errors and 16 as forgotten. For the UK group 8 memories received a score of zero, one of which was classed as an error and the remainder as forgotten. The distribution of error and forgotten responses for the non-UK group was very similar for consistency scores of 0.2–0.4, but shifted to predominantly forgotten responses for scores in the range 0.5–0.8. Of the very small number of memories ($n = 9$) falling at points 0.1–0.8 for the UK group, 7 were classed as forgotten and 2 as errors.

Error responses with consistency scores of zero are particularly interesting, as they may reflect the "wrong time slice" errors noted by Neisser and Harsch (1992). There seem to be a number of possibilities here. One is that a subject may have learned the news from a number of different sources in a number of different events—for example, heard it on the news, was subsequently told about it by a friend, and later read about it in a newspaper. At retrieval the subject is unable to discriminate which memory from a range of candidate memories actually represents the *original* learning episode and, when the wrong memory is selected, a wrong time-slice error occurs. Another possibility is that a subject may construct a memory (Conway, in press; Norman & Bobrow, 1979; Williams & Hollan, 1981). Given that the subjects know the original event actually happened and approximately when, then by searching memory, autobiographical knowledge relating to the specified period can be constructed into a "memory". Or, maybe, fragmentary knowledge accurately representing some attributes of the original memory is combined with other knowledge inferred to be part of the original experience. Unfortunately, the data in the present study do not discriminate between wrong time-slice errors and errors arising from inferential reconstruction. Nevertheless, the very detailed accounts classed as "error" memories with zero consistency scores in the non-UK group, suggests that the former type of wrong time-slice error is, perhaps, the more frequent error when a memory is completely incorrect at recall.

Other memories with consistency scores in the range 0.5–0.8 for the non-UK group and 0.1–0.8 for the UK group took the form of reconstructive errors. In such cases, a subject might misremember at retest that she had been in her *living room* when originally she had reported being in her *kitchen*, or a subject might report being in her *office* when earlier she had reported being in *the corridor outside her office*. Indeed, one of our subjects reported at retest watching a football game interrupted by the news, when originally he had reported watching a basketball game (see the discussion of Neisser, 1982, 1986, in Chapter 2). In general, these errors appeared to be schematised in the sense that the erroneous memory attributes introduced at retest were highly related to the attributes given in the original test.

In the pattern of errors, then, there is evidence of reconstruction of memory attributes and retrieval of the wrong memory. For the non-UK group, these errors were widespread and approximately one-third of all responses were counted as errors. For the UK subject group, errors were rare and accounted for less than 3% of responses. Instead, memories in the UK group were characterised by remarkable consistency and detail. More generally, FMs in both the UK and non-UK groups fit well with Brown and Kulik's account of FM reports containing detailed information concerning people, place, activity and source, and some "irrelevant" details not usually retained in autobiographical memories. Our subjects who met the FM memory criteria remembered details such as what they had for breakfast, what television programme they had been watching, the exact words spoken by a university lecturer, the place where someone had written the news on a wall and the name of the radio broadcaster who's show had been interrupted. Many subjects recalled even more specific details, such as "tying my shoelaces", "handing a five-pound note to a ticket vendor at a London Underground station" and "walking towards a mirror in a room as the news was announced on radio" (Conway et al., 1994, provide further examples of full FM memory descriptions). In short, the FMs identified in our subjects appeared to have the "live" quality emphasised by Brown and Kulik.

Having established the presence of FMs, the next step was to investigate the differential association of FMs and non-FMs with the encoding and rehearsal variables. Table 3.2 shows the distribution of subjects with and without FMs to each of the three points on each of the rating scales. Note that the scales are organised in four groups: affect, importance, prior knowledge, and rehearsal. Subjects with FMs had a reliably greater affective response, perceived the news as more personally and nationally important, and had more prior knowledge of, and interest in, the Thatcher governments, than subjects without FMs. Overall, the majority of subjects with FMs judged the news moderate to high on the affect, importance and prior knowledge variables, whereas the majority of subjects who did not have FMs judged the news moderate to low on these same variables. On the measures of rehearsal (note that the scale that assessed media rehearsal is here called "watched", because virtually all the subjects indicated that they had watched television coverage of the news and its aftermath), subjects with FMs reliably rehearsed the event more frequently on all three scales than subjects without FMs. These differences reflect the fact that FM subjects indicated moderate levels of rehearsal, whereas non-FM subjects indicated moderate to low levels of rehearsal.

TABLE 3.2
Mean Secondary Ratings for the FM and Non-FM Groups
(from Conway et al., 1994, table 1)

	FM Subjects			Non-FM Subjects		
	High	Moderate	Low	High	Moderate	Low
Affect						
Intensity	0.219	0.531	0.250	0.078	0.454	0.468
Surprise	0.566	0.359	0.075	0.390	0.475	0.135
Importance[a]						
PI	0.167	0.605	0.228	0.057	0.404	0.539
NI	0.715	0.254	0.031	0.482	0.468	0.500
Prior knowledge						
Knowledge	0.101	0.618	0.281	0.014	0.383	0.603
Interest	0.201	0.659	0.140	0.106	0.575	0.319
Rehearsal						
Thought	0.070	0.793	0.137	0.000	0.425	0.575
Spoke	0.044	0.666	0.290	0.000	0.345	0.645
Watched	0.123	0.746	0.131	0.035	0.517	0.448

[a] PI = personal importance, NI = national importance.

Not shown in Table 3.2 are data from the measure of "other memories", which were included in the "prior knowledge" group of variables. The other memories variable was scored 0 for no memories and 1 when any memories were named, and it was found that subjects with FMs spontaneously recalled reliably more other memories (mean = 0.56) than subjects without FMs (mean = 0.34). Thus, of all subjects with FMs, 56% were reminded of other events. The subjects recalled between one and four other memories and after examination of the protocols for the FM group these were classified into memories which featured political events, memories which featured only personal autobiographical events, and memories which featured both types of events. The distribution of other memories across these categories was political events 44%, autobiographical events 18% and mixtures of both the types of events 38%. For UK subjects, the political events which were recalled all related to occurrences during Margaret Thatcher's 11 years in power, such as the resignation of Chancellor Nigel Lawson, the Falklands War and the miners' strike, and a number of subjects recalled Thatcher's election to office in 1979 and her famous quotation from St. Francis when entering Number 10 Downing Street. The subjects in the non-UK group tended to recall more contemporaneous political events such as current wars and other political changes, particularly in Eastern Europe. Overall, then, the subjects with FMs were often spontaneously reminded (in Schank's, 1982, sense) of other events; these were usually political events and for UK subjects these related directly to Thatcher's political career. It is possible that this spontaneous recollection of related events may indicate the integration of a memory of the reception event with other long-term knowledge. Such integration might facilitate the stabilisation in long-term memory of knowledge structures representing thematic aspects of the political period dominated by Prime Minister Thatcher (Brown, 1990).

The subjects with FMs differed, then, from the subjects without FMs on all the secondary variables relating to encoding and rehearsal. In order to explore how these variables might be interrelated for the two groups, the data were entered into a structural equation analysis (Bentler, 1980; 1989; Bentler & Weeks, 1980). The purpose of structural equations is to find a theoretically interesting model that accounts for the variance in all the observed variables. In our model, we defined affect, importance, prior knowledge and rehearsal as latent factors, each consisting of the variables shown in Table 3.2 (note that prior knowledge also included the observed variable other memories). We then developed a model to account for the secondary variables in the FM group, the group of most interest to us. Our initial insight was that prior knowledge would be integral to memory formation and that without prior knowledge memories could not be formed. Thus we assumed that this construct would influence all other constructs.

Following Brown and Kulik, we then assumed that importance would be a critical factor and this would in part be determined by prior knowledge which would itself influence affect and rehearsal. Figure 3.8 shows the best fitting solution for the secondary ratings from the FM group. In Fig. 3.8, the latent constructs affect, importance, prior knowledge and rehearsal are shown in circles and the observed variables are shown in squares. The direction of the paths between the constructs and variables, indicated by the arrow heads, show significant contributions of the constructs to each other and to the observed variables. So, for example, the paths between knowledge/interest and the other three constructs show that this construct contributes significantly to all other constructs and, hence, indirectly to all measured variables. The greater the degree of knowledge/interest, the higher the levels of importance, affect and rehearsal. Importance, too, is positively associated with levels of affect and rehearsal, such that the more important an event the greater the affect and extent of rehearsal. Affect

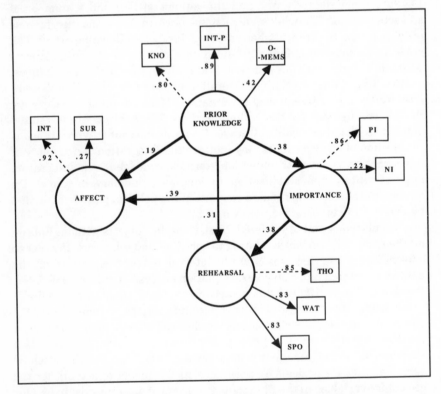

FIG. 3.8. Causal model of relations between secondary variables for the FM group (from Conway et al., 1994, fig. 3). Dashed lines denote fixed paths. All paths are significant ($P < 0.05$).

and rehearsal, however, were not found to be directly associated nor were they reciprocally related to knowledge/interest and importance. Thus, for FMs, knowledge/interest and importance act to determine the degree of affect and extent of rehearsal.

Having established this model, the next and crucial stage was to apply it to the secondary ratings for the non-FM group. If this model also fitted these data, then it could be concluded that the same constructs and processes mediate the formation of both FMs and non-FMs and any differences simply lie in the degree of affect, importance, prior knowledge and rehearsal. In this case, it could be confidently concluded that there is no special encoding of FMs. In contrast, if the FM secondary ratings model does not fit the non-FM secondary ratings, then this will indicate that the two types of memory are formed in different ways. For instance, the FMH argues that importance is a critical component in the formation of FMs but not in the formation of non-FMs. If this is correct, then it may be that the importance construct itself is not required in modelling the non-FM data or, possibly, that its relation to other constructs will change. When the FM model was fitted to the non-FM data, a significant discrepancy between the model and the data was observed and it was found that the two paths leading from the importance construct to the affect and rehearsal constructs were no longer significant. This shows that the construct importance does not play the same role in the formation of FMs and non-FMs. Accordingly, a new model was computed that omitted the paths from importance to affect and rehearsal and this model (shown in Fig. 3.9) was found to be a good fit for the non-FM secondary ratings. The conclusion of these analyses is that importance or personal consequentiality plays a central role in the formation of FMs but not in the formation of non-FMs, as predicted by the FMH.

Brown and Kulik (1977) summarised their conception of FM formation in a schematic flow chart that depicted how the various processes in memory formation functioned over the encoding period (see Fig. 1.5). In the light of our own findings, we proposed a modified version of their scheme and this is shown in Fig. 3.10. In Fig. 3.10, the formation of a memory is viewed as the culmination of a *sequence* of processes operating over time either separately or in conjunction. The first set of processes feature the utilisation of prior knowledge and these processes are common to the formation of all memories (see Figs 3.8 and 3.9). A second set of processes then evaluate the importance of the event and a third set of processes mediate the experience of affect in response to event features. When importance is high and comes to be associated with affect, then FMs are formed. Brown and Kulik proposed that importance had to reach or exceed levels of "biological significance" and we interpret this to mean that the item of news has to be judged as having consequences for self which

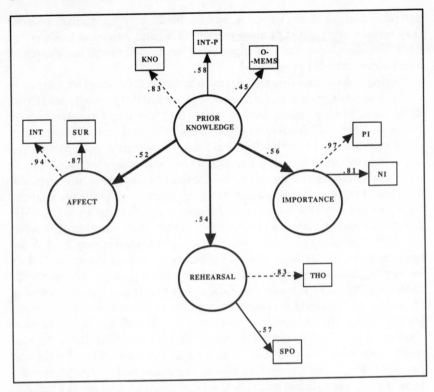

FIG. 3.9. Causal model of relations between secondary variables for the non-FM group (from Conway et al., 1994, fig. 4). Dashed lines denote fixed paths. All paths are significant ($P < 0.05$).

are *more* significant than the consequences typically assigned to most items of news. This was certainly the case for the majority of UK subjects in our study, for whom the resignation of Prime Minister Margaret Thatcher represented the end of an era in British politics. If, however, importance does not reach some putative critical level, then an association between affect and importance is not present and these processes then have separate effects upon memory formation. In our study, this latter case was found to lead to the formation of non-FMs.

Not shown in Fig. 3.10 are the direct effects of prior knowledge upon rates of rehearsal which were present for both FMs and non-FMs. Rehearsal rates were, in fact, very low for the non-FM group (mean ratings 2.6, indicating that many subjects did not rehearse the event) and at only moderate levels for the FM group (mean ratings 2.1). Nevertheless, this aspect of the findings demonstrates that subjects with greater prior knowledge were more likely to think and talk about the resignation and

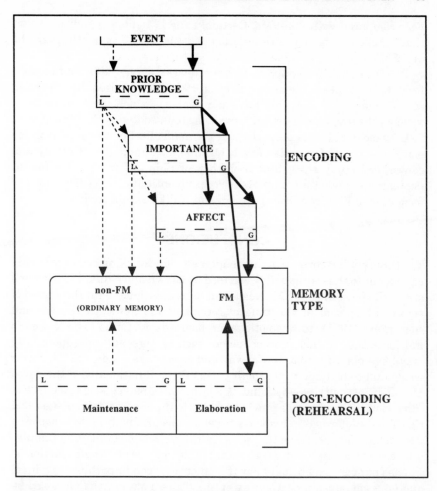

FIG. 3.10. Sequence of processes in memory formation and maintenance (from Conway et al., 1994, fig. 6). L, lesser; G, greater.

more likely to follow media reports of the resignation than subjects with lower levels of prior knowledge and interest and this was the case irrespective of type of memory (Figs 3.8 and 3.9). For the FM group only, there was also an additional effect of importance upon rates of rehearsal (see Fig. 3.8). Possibly this reflects the greater availability of FMs in memory generally. Perhaps memories of important events are accessed comparatively frequently in the period following the reception event and this occurs because of their associations with currently self-relevant themes, plans and goals. It is even feasible that this association between importance and rehearsal may reflect some differential consolidation of

FMs compared with non-FMs. Certainly, the FM subjects indicated that they "thought" about the resignation reliably more frequently than the non-FM subjects (see Table 3.2).

Finally, Fig. 3.10 also suggests that rehearsal serves different functions for different types of memories. For non-FMs it is proposed that the main role of rehearsal is in preventative maintenance, which acts to preserve in memory the fragmentary event-knowledge represented by these memories. In the case of FMs it is proposed that the main effect of rehearsal is in the elaboration of FM reports. Taken together the findings of Conway and co-workers' study show that frequency of FMs differs across different populations and that importance/consequentiality is critical in the formation of FMs, confirming Brown and Kulik's earlier findings

CONCLUSIONS

The three studies covered in this chapter all found striking evidence of FMs equivalent to those originally described by Brown and Kulik. In Pillemer's study, the formation of FMs was found to be associated with the degree of emotional arousal at the time of receipt of the news. In Neisser and co-workers' (1991) study, emotional arousal was not found to be related to FM formation, although other factors such as personal consequentiality may have played a role. In Conway and co-workers' study, the key factor was found to be importance, both personally and nationally, of the news, although intensity of emotional experience also played some role in FM formation. These findings provide support to the general claim of the FMH that FMs are formed in response to conditions arising from first learning surprising and consequential news. In their specific details, the findings are less conclusive and suggest that FMs may arise when emotion is intense but consequentiality low (Pillemer) or when importance is critical and emotion subsidiary (Conway et al.). Thus, FMs may be mediated by importance and/or by emotion. Rehearsal, however, was not found in any of the studies to be associated with FM formation and this further suggests that factors influencing encoding are critical in the generation of FMs.

CHAPTER FOUR

"Real" Flashbulb Memories and Flashbulb Memories Across the Lifespan

One of the advantages of studying FMs associated with the announcement of public news is that large numbers of subjects can be identified some of whom, as we saw in the preceding chapter, may have FMs to the same item of news. Groups of subjects with and without FMs can then be contrasted (e.g. Brown & Kulik, 1977; Conway et al., 1994; Neisser, et al., 1991) and memory consistency can be tracked over time (e.g. Christianson, 1989; McCloskey et al., 1988; Pillemer, 1984). Despite these and other advantages, it is evident that there are very few public events which give rise to widespread formation of FMs. Instead, FMs are more frequently associated with private and personal events such as the "personal shock" category of events sampled by Brown and Kulik. Indeed, Brown and Kulik found that FMs for personal shocks were among the most detailed and durable of the range of FMs examined in their study (see Fig. 1.1). Sampling FMs for public events is, then, mainly a convenience, and although it does ensure at least some knowledge of the stimulus event, the majority of FMs—"real" FMs—must occur in response to more idiographic events experienced by individuals rather than groups. This chapter considers findings from studies investigating a wider range of FMs and, from the perspective of the FMH, we will be particularly interested in whether the key encoding factors of surprise and personal consequentiality also play a role in this much more diverse sample of FMs.

PERSONAL FLASHBULB MEMORIES

In a study by Rubin and Kozin (1984), 58 undergraduate students described their three most vivid memories and then rated each memory on 7-point scales, including scales for national importance, personal importance, surprise, personal consequentiality, vividness, change in ongoing activity, emotional change and rehearsal. Memories were also dated. Of the 174 memories, 31 were concerned with accidents and injuries, 20 related to sports events, 18 referred to encounters with the opposite sex, 16 featured animals/pets, 9 were of deaths, 9 were of events occurring in the first week at college, 9 related to vacations, 5 involved public appearances and 5 related to incidents which had occurred when the subjects were at school. Fifty-two of the memories could not be classified and, importantly, over the whole sample only four memories were associated with news events. In order to check that these were in fact FMs, the number of canonical categories in each memory was counted and out of a possible total of 6 a mean of 4.5 with a range of 2–6 was observed. These figures far exceed Brown and Kulik's criteria for scoring a FM and, moreover, 71% of the memories were identified as containing the sort of vivid, idiosyncratic detail typically found in FMs. This then is unambiguous evidence that FMs to public news are rare compared with the incidence of FMs to personal, autobiographical events.

The rating scale most strongly associated with these FMs was that of personal importance. Other scales for surprise, personal consequentiality, change in ongoing activity, change in emotion and rehearsal rate, were not found to be systematically associated with the memories. Thus, the two key factors of the FMH, surprise and personal consequentiality, did not appear to be critical in this sample of FMs. However, Rubin and Kozin did not report the correlations in detail and so it is not known whether there was some small but reliable correlation between these ratings and memory vividness. It certainly seems from their figure 1 (Rubin & Kozin, 1984, p. 89) that there would have been a positive correlation between surprise and memory vividness and, possibly, between change in emotion and vividness. Partly in an attempt to investigate this more directly, Rubin and Kozin also had their subjects recall memories to a list of 20 cues selected on the basis of a pilot study so as to elicit FMs and non-FMs with about equal frequency. Table 4.1 shows the full list of cues and the proportions of subjects classified as recalling FMs to each one.

The subjects again rated these memories, this time on the scales for consequentiality, surprise, emotional change and rehearsal. FMs were rated reliably higher on all these scales than non-FMs, implicating both FMH and rehearsal variables in FMs. It is curious, however, that Rubin and Kozin did not collect ratings of personal importance for these cued FMs

TABLE 4.1
Percentage of FMs and Non-FMs to 20 Cues
(from Rubin & Kozin, 1984, table 1)

Cue	FM	Non-FM
The night of your high school graduation	82.5	17.5
An accident you were in or witnessed	82.0	18.0
First meeting with your roommate	81.1	18.9
The night of your senior prom	77.2	21.8
Giving a public speech	69.8	30.2
When you received your university acceptance	64.3	35.7
Your first date	58.2	41.8
An early romantic experience	58.2	41.8
Attempted assassination of President Reagan	50.0	50.0
The resignation of President Nixon	40.0	60.0
First time you flew in an airplane	38.5	61.5
The moment you opened your SAT scores	32.7	67.3
Your 17th birthday	29.8	70.2
The first space shuttle flight	24.5	75.5
The last time you ate a holiday dinner at home	23.2	76.8
First class at university	21.4	78.6
Assassination of President Sadat	21.4	78.6
The attempted assassination of the Pope	21.0	79.0
First time your parents left you alone	18.9	81.1
Your 13th birthday	12.5	87.5

given the close association between this and FMs from the first part of their study. It is also notable that the actual overall mean ratings for FMs on consequentiality (3.54), surprise (3.69), emotional change (4.07) and rehearsal (3.76), are all below or at the mid-point on the 7-point scale, indicating only moderate to low levels of consequentiality, surprise, emotional change and rehearsal. Thus, although FMs were found to differ reliably from non-FMs, it could not be claimed that particularly high values were registered on any of the scales.

Finally, for both sets of memories, the subjects rated the likelihood of occurrence of the remembered event. Interestingly, the subjective probability of occurrence was not found to be related to either FMs or ratings of surprise. It can be seen from Table 4.1 that the majority of cues associated with the recall of FMs refer to events, which are highly predictable and which would, in many cases, have been actively anticipated. Nevertheless, for cued recall of FMs, surprise was reliably associated with the incidence of FMs, such that the more surprising an event the more likely a FM and, as noted above, there was some suggestion of a similar association between surprise and memory vividness in the free recall of the three most vivid memories. Flashbulb memory researchers have often assumed that for an event to lead to FM formation, that event must be surprising in the sense that its likelihood of occurrence is low. Rubin and Kozin's findings contradict this assumption and demonstrate that events can be surprising, and lead to FM formation, even when the subjective probability of occurrence is high. Events can be surprising in many ways (e.g. because expectations are not fulfilled, because a predicted event turns out to contain a surprising feature, etc.) and in the FMs sampled in Rubin and Kozin's study, it would appear that these other sources of surprise were more critical to FM formation than the probability of occurrence of events.

The central finding of Rubin and Kozin's study is that by far the majority of FMs are formed to personally important life-events rather than newsworthy events of national and international importance. These "real" FMs are not generally associated with personal consequentiality and, as Rubin and Kozin point out, an event that leads to FM formation can have few consequences and yet be personally important. Despite these claims, it should be noted that the second part of their study found moderate levels of personal consequentiality to be significantly related to FMs. Following on from Rubin and Kozin's paper, Conway and Bekerian (1988) wondered whether there might not be yet other types of FMs which were *wholly* unrelated to any of the variables of personal importance, consequentiality, surprise, emotional change and rehearsal. The impetus for this arose from related studies of autobiographical memory (Conway & Bekerian, 1987) in which subjects occasionally recalled highly detailed and vivid memories which were judged to be low in personal importance. In Conway and Bekerian's (1988) study, subjects recalled one memory which was of no particular importance and another memory which was instructed to be of high personal importance. For each memory, a FM questionnaire similar to that used by Rubin and Kozin (1984) was completed. Memories of personally important events had a mean vividness rating of 5.8, which was significantly higher than the mean vividness rating of 5.1 for memories of unimportant events. Nevertheless, mean ratings of 5 and higher indicate the recall of highly vivid memories for both personally important and unimportant events. The data were further analysed in series of regressions and it was found that consequentiality, emotionality and rehearsal, all correlated uniquely and significantly with the rated memory vividness of personally important events. For unimportant events, however, only ratings of change in ongoing activities predicted memory vividness. This suggests that some highly vivid flashbulb-type memories are not associated with any of the factors previously thought to influence FM formation and duration. The vivid memories of events low in personal importance were of mundane everyday events such as becoming mildly ill, going on a trip, playing a sport, going on holiday, etc. These types of events may involve moderate changes or divergences in daily/yearly routines and, perhaps, for this reason are retained in some detail (see Chapter 6).

For "real" FMs, it appears that consequentiality, personal importance and emotion are important factors in memory formation. However, the particular mix of these factors in the generation of individual FMs is variable and one factor may dominate at the expense of the others (as in the first part of Rubin and Kozin's study). In a series of important studies by Pillemer and his colleagues (Pillemer, Goldsmith, Panter, & White, 1988; Pillemer, Rinehart, & White, 1986), emotion was found to be the critical factor in FM formation. Pillemer et al. (1986) investigated students' memories for their first year at university. Subjects drawn from a college undergraduate population recalled four distinct memories from their first year at college which they fully described and for each memory they completed a questionnaire similar to that used by Pillemer (1984; see Chapter 3). The memory descriptions were coded and classified into specific and general memories and it was found that over 87% referred to "one-moment-in-time" incidents. These descriptions contained a pattern of canonical categories indicative of FMs and Pillemer et al. illustrate this with the following example memory description:

> My first memory is of a woman I dated who lived in my dorm (she graduated). I met her in a show we both did, and the distinct picture I have is the two of us alone in the dining room, about 8 pm, really talking for the first time. I was wearing a yellow sweatshirt and red shorts, she a lavender/white striped blouse and a lavender skirt. She always wore skirts and I always wore shorts or jeans. We compared backgrounds—though we live within 1 hr. from each other, our childhoods were incredibly different. The scene seems to symbolise our relationship. (Pillemer et al., 1986, p. 112)

The memory descriptions were further classified into four groups of memories relating to educational activities (academic memories), romance memories, housing memories (relating to student accommodation) and recreation memories. Recreation memories formed the largest class and academic memories the smallest (19%). The majority of memory descriptions referred to social interactions with others and very few featured only the rememberer. Thus, the pattern of event recall by students in this study was broadly similar to that reported by Rubin and Kozin (1984).

The rememberer's own emotions were referred to in 84% of the descriptions and 47% mentioned emotions experienced by others. Analysis of the rating scales found that emotion was rated significantly higher than all other measures (i.e. surprise, life impact, etc.) and, moreover, a cluster of measures relating to emotional experience was found to be the best predictor of ratings of memory clarity (vividness). Also of interest was the finding that rehearsal was not related to memory clarity and 26% of memories were rated as never having been talked about before. Finally, all subjects recalled memories from the first part of their first term at college and this was unrelated to how well prepared subjects judged they had been for college. In other studies, Pillemer et al. (1986) observed a very similar pattern of findings and, taken together, their results provide strong evidence that emotion (either negative or positive) is a critical factor in the formation of FMs during life transitions such as the transition from high school to college.

In a subsequent study, Pillemer et al. (1988) extended their research programme to college alumnae who had taken their degree 2, 12 and 22 years previously. As in the earlier study, the alumnae recalled four memories from their first year at college and completed the FM questionnaire. Memories were generally found to be from the early part of the year, often from the first day, and referred to first-time experiences. They featured interactions with others and were associated with the experience of various emotions, both positive and negative. Indeed, higher levels of emotion were characteristic of these memories, whereas surprise and rehearsal were at moderate to low levels. However, one difference from the earlier study was that intensity of emotion at the time of an event and perceived life impact, also at the time of an event, were found to be significant predictors of memory clarity. Note that this pattern of findings was the same for all three groups. Thus, "life impact" or personal consequentiality *at the time of an event* can be associated with personal FMs, although in both studies intensity of emotion was the more consistent predictor.

More recently, Pillemer, Picariello, Law, and Reichman (in press b) reported a study in which they investigated memories for events that had occurred during the course of individuals' first degree and which were judged to be influential in some way. The corpus of memories described many events that proved critical in forming or changing the academic course pursued by the graduates. Many of these memories had been retained over long periods of time and were highly vivid and flashbulb in nature. As an example of this class of memories for influential events from university, Pillemer et al. (in press b) cite the following memory recounted by the noted developmental psychologist Jerome Kagan, who originally started reading chemistry rather then psychology:

My commitment to chemistry was further weakened by a psychology professor's idle comment in the introductory psychology course. He had posed a question I cannot remember, but to which I apparently gave a good answer. He asked me to stay and as we walked across the campus he said I had an apperceptive feeling for psychology and added, "You would probably be a good psychologist". The sentence rings as clearly now as it did that afternoon twenty-two years ago. (Kagan, 1972, p. 140)

Kagan's memory is, however, by no means atypical and Pillemer et al. (in press b) report many memories of a similar quality for students from a wide range of disciplines and who did not necessarily proceed to eminence in their chosen field. As a further example, consider this account from a young graduate student:

My first Shakespeare class ... would have to rank as one of my most influential experiences, since it started me on the life I'm following now (graduate school in Elizabethan literature). But the memory I have from that class is very small and tight. Oh well. Although I have good feelings and good memories about the entire class (1st Semester of sophomore year) I remember the first day best. I was fascinated by the easy way (the professor) roamed through Shakespeare, by just the amount of knowledge he had. He seemed to know everything. In fact, after class, I asked him if he could identify a quote I had found about fencing "Keep up your bright swords, for the dew will rust them." Immediately he said "Othello, Act 1, Scene 2 I believe." Which turned out to be exactly right. I wanted to know a body of literature that well. I'm still working on it. (Pillemer et al., in press b, p. 20)

Of course, many of the memories were not of events relating to academic activities but rather referred to the adaptation to university life, the creation of a social network, and to personal relationships. Nevertheless, the memories were highly vivid and appeared to serve what Pillemer et al. (in press b) call a "directive" function. That is to say that the events retained in FM-like detail often marked points at which a major life plan was initiated or, in some cases, abandoned. In Chapter 6, this relation between plans, goals and FMs is explored in further detail.

In an unpublished study, Conway (1988), following on from the work of Pillemer and his colleagues, investigated undergraduates' memories for their first week at university. In this study, groups of first- and final-year subjects recalled five "college" memories to cues that specified events all students would have experienced in their first week at university. The subjects recalled, described and rated their memories on a FM questionnaire within 1 month of the start of term and again 4 months later.

At test and retest, the subjects also recalled five other memories, not related to university, from any part of their lives, and these too were described and rated on the questionnaire. Figure 4.1 shows the mean vividness ratings for each group. Associations between vividness and the ratings of surprise, consequentiality, etc., were assessed in a series of multiple regressions. For the first-year students recalling memories within 1 month of the start of term, no single variable was found to uniquely predict memory vividness. Four months later, however, ratings of emotional intensity, change in ongoing activity and personal importance,

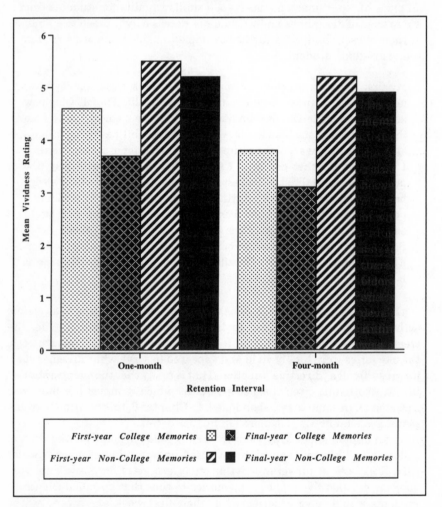

FIG. 4.1. Mean vividness ratings for college and non-college memories at two retention intervals (from Conway, 1988).

all correlated uniquely and positively with memory vividness. For this group of first-year students, memory vividness actually decreased over the 4-month retention interval (see Fig. 4.1), and this parallels the finding by Wright (1993; discussed in Chapter 3) of changes in personal importance and emotion over the initial few months of retention. This aspect of Conway's (1988) findings perhaps suggests that only durable vivid memories, FMs, are associated with factors such as emotion, change in activities and personal importance.

For the final-year students, emotional intensity at the 1-month retention interval and emotional intensity and rehearsal at the 4-month retention interval were found to correlate significantly and positively with memory vividness. In the case of these more experienced students, who were not going through the transition from school to university, it may be that events at the start of term integrate with pre-existing long-term memory knowledge structures and so factors such as emotional experience at the time of an event can determine memory vividness (cf. Conway, 1988). Finally, non-college memories in both groups were significantly more vivid than the college memories and emotional intensity and personal consequentiality were found to be significant predictors initially, although only emotional intensity was significantly correlated with memory vividness at the 4-month delay. For these highly vivid memories, emotional intensity was, then, the more consistent predictor.

Another period of transition which is also associated with the formation of FMs, and confined solely to females, is the first menstruation or menarche. Pillemer, Koff, Rinehart, and Rierdan (1987) sampled 99 female college students who completed both a FM questionnaire and the Menstrual Distress Questionnaire (Moos, 1977). One of the aims of this study was to examine associations between preparedness for the menarche and memory clarity. Women who are less well prepared suffer more from menstrual distress than those who are well prepared, and the increased emotion associated with increased menstrual distress should give rise to more detailed memories. Pillemer et al. (1987) found that this was in fact the case and women who were not well prepared provided far more vivid and detailed accounts of their first menstruation than women who were better prepared. Indeed, some women in their sample who menstruated late and as a consequence had consulted doctors and been fairly extensively educated on the time of likely occurrence and what to expect, rarely remembered their first menstruation. Thus, the degree of surprise at the the experience and the extent of emotional distress were found to be critical factors in the formation of FMs for the menarche.

Personal importance, emotional intensity and, occasionally, personal consequentiality, have all been found to be reliably associated with "real" FMs. One striking feature of "real" FMs is that they often refer to first-time experiences and this was the case in all the studies discussed above. First-time experiences (FEMs) feature in autobiographical memory more generally (cf. Conway, 1990; 1993; Conway & Rubin, 1993) and have recently been studied directly by Robinson (1992). Robinson (1992) examined memory for what he called "mini-histories", such as memory for a first romantic relationship and memory for learning to drive a car. The central finding of Robinson's study was that mini-histories were structured around FMs for critical moments in the history and these critical moments were of highly self-relevant FEMs such as "first kiss" and "first time driving a car". Indeed, for learning to drive a car, all subjects gave highly detailed descriptions of the first time they drove a car alone and these descriptions featured self-evaluative and emotional attributes. First-time experiences may, then, be a special class of events that, because of their relevance for self and the emotion they engender and, perhaps, because of their uniqueness (surprise value) and their consequences, give rise to a high incidence of FMs.

TRAUMATIC FLASHBULB MEMORIES

Brown and Kulik speculated that when an event caused excessive levels of surprise and emotion, then this could lead to retrograde amnesia rather than the formation of highly accessible and detailed FMs. It seems that on this point Brown and Kulik were incorrect (see Chapter 2) and recent work has documented FMs arising from traumatic events featuring strong emotional experience often associated with intense shock or other extreme forms of surprise. Yuille and Cutshall (1986), in one of the best field studies of a traumatic event, investigated witnesses' memories of a robbery compounded by a fatal shooting. The event took place on a spring afternoon outside a gun shop. The robber had entered the shop, tied up the owner, and taken some money and guns. The owner managed to free himself and collected his own gun prior to leaving the shop to take the licence number of the robber's car. But the robber had not entered his car and a face-to-face confrontation between the robber and shop owner then took place. The two men were standing about 6 feet apart when the robber fired two shots at the store owner. The store owner returned the robber's fire and discharged all six shots from his own gun killing the robber. The store owner survived the incident. Twenty-one witnesses viewed the event, some from the street itself, others from nearby buildings, and yet others from passing cars.

Fifteen of the witnesses were interviewed on the same day at the scene of the crime and the remaining six witnesses were interviewed within 2 days. Four to five months later, Yuille and Cutshall were able to re-interview 13 of the 21 witnesses and all these were major witnesses who had been near to the shooting and had seen most of the event. The first interview was conducted by officers of the Royal Canadian Mounted Police following a set procedure. The witnesses first provided a free description of their memory for the shooting and then answered questions aimed at amplifying aspects of the event. This same procedure with slight modifications (see Yuille & Cutshall, 1986, p. 293) was followed in the retest interviews. Responses from the two interviews were classified into the three categories of *action, people* and *objects*. Note that all subjects provided responses in all categories; thus by any of the criteria used to score a memory account as a FM (see Chapters 1 and 2), all of these subjects would have been credited with FMs for the shooting. A detailed account of the incident was constructed on the basis of forensic evidence, photographs from the scene of the crime, confiscated objects, stolen articles, agreements on details between witness accounts, reports from members of the emergency services, autopsy and medical reports, and a re-enactment of the incident. Witness accuracy at original interview and again at test was then determined by comparing the interview responses against the constructed account.

Figure 4.2 shows the percentages of correct responses in each of the three categories for both interviews. It can be seen from Fig. 4.2 that on both occasions the witnesses were highly accurate about details of the actions, other people and the objects that featured in the crime. Further analyses indicated that changes in accuracy were minor over the two interviews and most witnesses provided consistently accurate reports in both interviews. Indeed, the level of accuracy, 80% plus, is highly comparable to the consistency in memory reports observed in the FM studies described in Chapter 3. One potential problem is that Yuille and Cutshall's findings are, of course, based on only one event, and it may be that some unidentified aspect of this event gave rise to the formation of accurate, detailed and durable memories. This, however, seems unlikely in the light of additional findings by Fisher, Geiselman, and Amador (1989), who examined memory accuracy for a set of 24 different events that had featured various crimes and which were subsequently investigated by the police. Across the 24 events, Fisher et al. identified 325 facts that could be corroborated against other sources of evidence and found that 94% of these were accurately reported by witnesses. This suggests that events which feature crimes— often violent crimes—give rise to a high incidence of FM formation (note that it does not follow from this that witness memory is necessarily *correct* on *all* memory details; see the analyses of errors reported by Yuille & Cutshall, 1986).

Finally, although Yuille and Cutshall did not examine rehearsal rates, they did attempt to measure stress levels on a self-assessed 7-point scale. Five of the subjects indicated high levels of stress during the incident and reported sleep disturbances in the days following the shooting. Mean

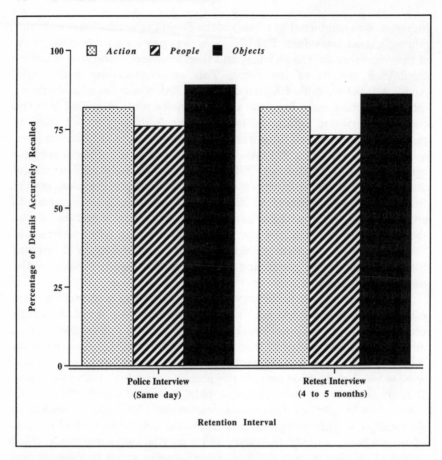

FIG. 4.2. Mean percentages of accurately recalled details of a crime (data from Yuille & Cutshall, 1986, table 3).

accuracy for this sub-group was 93.36% in the police interview and 88.24% at retest. In contrast, the remainder of the witnesses indicated low levels of stress and for this sub-group mean accuracy in the police interview and at retest was 75.13 and 75.88%, respectively. Both of these latter means were found to be significantly lower than mean accuracy in the stressed group. These findings lend further support to the claim that intense emotion is an important factor in the formation of FMs.

The intense emotions associated with traumatic events do not always lead immediately to highly accessible FMs. For example, Christianson and Nilsson (1989) report a single case study of a rape victim (C.M.) who developed a dense retrograde amnesia both for the assault and for her previous life. In fact, C.M. was able to recall a few extremely detailed aspects of the event without apparently being able to explain how these related to the event or why they had come to mind. The attack had taken place while C.M. was out jogging and a distinctive pattern of brickwork close by where the rape took place was remembered with extreme clarity. Some months after the assault, C.M. was again out jogging at a different location when a similar pattern of brickwork unexpectedly cued full retrieval of FMs for the rape; at the same time C.M.'s retrograde amnesia also lifted. This type of automatic and spontaneous cued recall following trauma is not uncommon—although a period of transient global amnesia apparently is—and individuals who have survived traumatic experiences often adopt patterns of behaviour explicitly designed to avoid encountering cues that would trigger the recall of FMs of the incident.

Directly experiencing trauma is far more stressful and emotional than, for instance, witnessing a crime, and the effects are more marked and far-reaching. Thus, traumatic events experienced in childhood have long been associated with a wide range of psychiatric disorders in later life. One characteristic of such disorders is the recall of highly vivid visual memories. Terr (1979; 1983) found that a group of children aged 5–14 years involved in a group kidnapping had full and detailed memories for the event at 1 and 4–5 years later. Some of these children had misperceived aspects of the event and so showed some "errors" in their recall and some incorrectly recalled specific perceptual details. However, all these traumatised children were able to provide highly detailed accounts, which were apparently accurate and which were based on vivid visual memories.

Memory for childhood traumas, however, is at least partly determined by the nature of the trauma—whether it is a single or repeated event—and Terr (1991) argued for two types of pathology associated with childhood trauma: one arising from a single negative event (type I trauma) and the other from repeated traumatic episodes (type II trauma), the latter usually being associated with child abuse. Following both types of trauma, a central characteristic of subsequent psychogenic illness is the recall, usually cued but sometimes intrusive, of strongly visual memories in which the child *resees* an episode of trauma. Type I traumas give rise to memories of the single event that are remarkably detailed and which appear to be, in Terr's (1991) words, "etched-in memories". Terr (1991, p. 14) comments that "Verbal recollections of single shocks in an otherwise trauma-free childhood are delivered in an amazingly clear and detailed fashion. Children sometimes sound like robots as they strive to tell every detail as efficiently as possible". It should be noted that the nature of the events associated with type I trauma are extreme, horrifying and often life-threatening, and in this respect clearly differ from the sorts of FM-events described earlier. Terr provides a number of detailed accounts and the following report typifies the type of extreme experience associated with type I trauma:

The first time that he visited the psychiatrist, a 5-year-old boy minutely described his stepfather's murder of his baby brother. The incident had occurred 2 weeks earlier. The boy knew just where under the television table in a motel room he had been hiding. He reported exactly where he had been sitting and lying before taking cover. He described the types of blows that fell upon his younger sibling and meticulously repeated the attacker's phrases and threats. He said that he had been trying to forget all this but he could not. (Terr, 1991, pp. 14–15)

In contrast, type II traumas give rise to more fragmentary memories and are associated with a different pattern of post-trauma symptoms. Nevertheless, detailed FM-like memories are present here too, although in this case there are obviously more memories, and as these arise from repeated abuse they often appear to form a sort of mini-history such as that discussed by Robinson (1992). Walker (1992) provides a number of detailed accounts by survivors of child sex abuse and repeated violence in which specific and highly detailed memories are described along with more schematic and conceptual accounts of the sequences of abuses. A typical account was given by one of Walker's clients, Louise, who was repeatedly abused by her father:

There are a lot of very dark and angry memories, but only in snatches. One is of being hungry and asking for a sandwich. My father said to me "If you ask again I'm going to put you in the bath". I did. I was hungry. And he picked me up and put me in the bath. I think he put my head under the water, but I can't remember now. I remember screaming and holding on to him, shouting "I love you! I love you! I love you! Please stop!" and him pushing my arms away and pushing me in again. (Walker, 1992, p. 36)

The vivid recall of memories of traumatic events in general is very common and has been identified as a central characteristic of Post-Traumatic Stress Disorder (PTSD). The American Psychiatric Association's (1986) *Diagnostic and Statistical Manual of Mental Disorders* (DSM-IIIR) specifies that one of the criteria for diagnosis of PTSD is that the traumatic event(s) must be persistently repeated in one of the following ways:

1. Recurrent and intrusive distressing recollections of the event.
2. Recurrent distressing dreams of the event.
3. Sudden acting or feeling as if the traumatic event were recurring (includes a sense of reliving the experience, illusions, hallucinations, and dissociative [flashback] episodes).
4. Intense psychological distress at exposure to events that symbolise or resemble an aspect of the traumatic event.

Horowitz and Reidbord (1992; Horowitz, Wilner, Kaltreider, & Alvarez, 1980) found that 90% of large and diverse groups of PTSD patients reported frequent and intense recall of traumatic events. Foy (1992) reports PTSD rates of 30–50% among Vietnam veterans, 45% in a sample of battered women, 50% in sexually abused children, 65% in adult survivors of childhood sexual abuse and 35% in rape victims. Thus, traumatic events often lead to the formation of detailed FM-like memories and for PTSD patients such memories are a major feature of the disorder.

Tragic and harrowing traumatic events sometimes featuring extreme threats to self are associated with a high incidence of FMs. However, by the very nature of these events, it is often not possible to check memory accuracy or consistency, nor is it feasible to collect the types of secondary measures of surprise, personal importance, etc., typically taken in more "traditional" FM studies, such as those reviewed in earlier chapters. The one exception to this is Yuille and Cutshall's (1986) study, and although they found memory to be remarkably accurate and detailed, they also found a low but distinct error rate for some event details. As noted in earlier chapters, this is not particularly surprising as FMs are not complete records, and so even in the case of an event of extreme trauma it is not expected that all details will be remembered. Event details that are not retained may be inferred or reconstructed in some other way when a FM account is given, and it must therefore be assumed that vivid accounts of traumatic events will contain at least some errors. More serious errors in accounts of traumatic events, such as the complete fabrication of a "memory" or a set of "memories", may occur when recall is elicited during the course of therapy, and Loftus (1993; see also Loftus & Kaufman, 1992) provides a timely reminder that FM accounts of traumatic events should not be taken at face value, particularly when these emerge suddenly after long periods of "repression". However, completely fabricated memories are probably comparatively rare and it would seem unlikely that, for example, the very large number of PTSD patients reporting detailed FMs for a diversity of traumatic events all fabricated their memories (see also Brewin, Andrews, & Gotlib, 1993; Christianson, 1992). More common, perhaps, is some low but persistent level of inferential errors for event details that were not retained in the first place.

FLASHBULB MEMORIES ACROSS THE LIFESPAN

One interesting feature of Brown and Kulik's (1977) original study was that some of their subjects would have been children when events such as the assassination of JFK occurred. Nevertheless, these same subjects provided flashbulb accounts; indeed, Kulik described his own childhood memory of learning of the assassination (see Chapter 1). In contrast, the subjects in Yarmey and Bull's (1978) FM study of the JFK assassination who were older than 54 years in 1963 when the assassination occurred showed a lower incidence of FMs (64%) than younger subjects (95%) aged between 11 and 54 years in 1963. These age differences suggest the intriguing possibility that there may be a systematic age gradient in the formation of FMs. In order to investigate the developmental aspect of this age gradient, Winograd and Killinger (1978) systematically sampled the memories of groups of subjects who differed in age at the time of occurrence of various events thought to promote FM formation. Subjects completed a FM questionnaire similar to that used by Brown and Kulik (1977) and here we will focus mainly on FMs for the JFK assassination, rather than other events which were also sampled by Winograd and Killinger (1978). Figure 4.3 shows the proportion of subjects classified as having FMs according to Brown and Kulik's original criteria—a positive response to the question "Do you recall your personal circumstances when you learned of ...?" and mention of at least one of the canonical categories (see Chapter 1).

It can be seen from Fig. 4.3 that there is a linear relationship between the proportion of subjects with FMs and age at the time of the assassination. The mid-point of the curve occurs when subjects were aged between 4 and 5 years and virtually all subjects aged 7 years at the time of the assassination were able to recall some aspects of the reception event in which they learned of the assassination.

Figure 4.4 shows the mean number of canonical categories recalled by subjects of different ages for all those subjects classed as having FMs. Here there is a clear disjunction at age 4–5 years such that subjects 5 years and older at the time of the assassination recalled more than subjects 4 years and younger. There are a number of possible explanations for these developmental age effects, one of which, considered by Winograd and Killinger, is that older subjects would have been at school when the news was announced—indeed, the memory descriptions confirm that this was in fact the case. The disruption of the school routine, typified by Brown and Kulik's FM account, was common for these subjects and it may have been this interruption of the school day that facilitated the formation of a distinctive memory. However, Winograd and Killinger are sceptical of this explanation, as in a parallel investigation of older subjects' recall of learning of the bombing of Pearl Harbor, they had observed a similar age-related growth in the incidence of FMs. But the announcement of the bombing had occurred on a Sunday afternoon and so was unlikely to have led to the disruption of any formal routines.

Other aspects of Winograd and Killinger's study are also of interest. For example, they found only a weak relation between rehearsal and FM accounts and conclude that rehearsal does not offer a particularly compelling

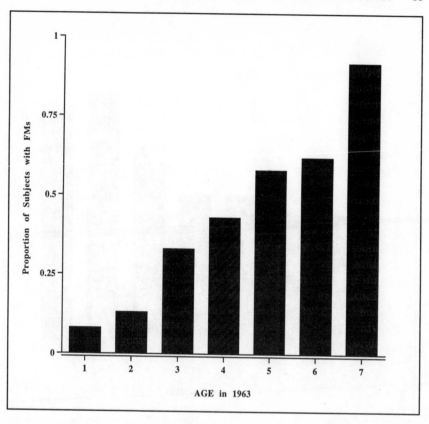

FIG. 4.3. Proportion of subjects of different ages with FMs for the JFK assassination (after Winograd & Killinger, 1983, fig. 2).

account of their findings. They also observed a high incidence of FMs to the resignation of Richard Nixon, a long expected event, and argued that surprise—in the sense of surprise at the occurrence of an event—cannot explain the formation of these FMs. Finally, they replicated Brown and Kulik's finding of a low incidence of FMs among White Americans for the assassination of the Black civil rights campaigner Martin Luther King. These findings, then, question the rehearsal account of FM formation and would seem to rule out a simple surprise account. Nonetheless, Winograd and Killinger favoured an account in terms of elaborative encoding and proposed that the developmental trend they had observed, of increasing incidence of FMs with increasing age at news reception, reflects the emerging understanding of the child. Older children are better placed to appreciate the significance of important public events and have long-term knowledge structures that facilitate understanding and encoding.

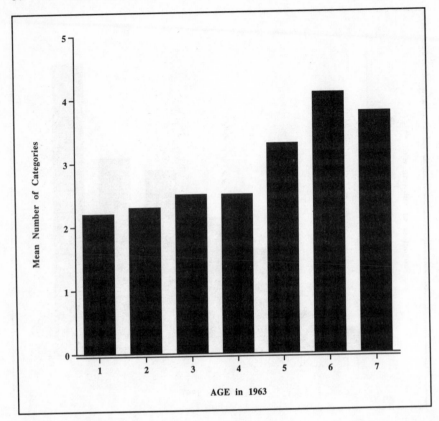

FIG. 4.4. Mean number of canonical categories recalled by subjects of different ages (after Winograd & Killinger, 1983, fig. 3).

Pillemer (1992a) conducted an intriguing study into children's memory for an unusual, naturally occurring event. The children in this study were attending a preschool and one group consisted of 3½-year-olds and a second group 4½-year-olds. While the children were in their classes, smoke from some cooking popcorn in the basement set off the fire alarm and following the fire drill the children were evacuated to their playgrounds while the fire service and police arrived. In fact no damage resulted and the children returned to their classes fairly promptly. Thus, the event although novel (for the children) and surprising was not traumatic and entailed no enduring or significant personal consequences. Two weeks later, the two groups of children were interviewed and asked open-ended questions about the event and specific questions about features of the event.

Figure 4.5 shows the proportions of all children providing information on five canonical categories. It can be seen from Fig. 4.5 that all the children

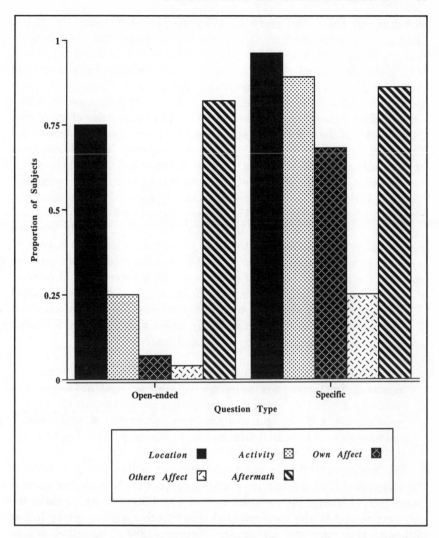

FIG. 4.5. Proportions of subjects recalling five canonical categories (data from Pillemer, 1992, table 6.1).

had comparatively detailed memories for the event and that the cues available in the specific questions were more effective in eliciting information than the open-ended questions. There were, however, some interesting age differences. For example, although many of the children were able to provide an answer to the question about their location when they heard the fire alarm, more than half the younger group (55%) placed themselves outside the school building in the playground. In contrast, virtually all the older group of 4½-year-olds (94%) correctly placed themselves inside the school. As Pillemer (1992) points out, there is some ambiguity about this finding, as the children once evacuated did indeed wait in the playground where they listened to the fire alarm. However, they *first* heard the alarm when inside the school. Also of interest was the finding that 75% of the older children but only 33% of the younger children described the sense of urgency associated with the evacuation of the school. Finally, 44% of the older group spontaneously mentioned the cause of the fire alarm compared with only 8% of the younger group. It would seem from these findings that although both sets of children had detailed memories for the event, only the older group had coherent and structured memories. This conclusion was lent further support in a 7-year follow-up in which the children, now aged 10 years and over, were re-interviewed at the preschool (Pillemer, Picariello, & Pruett, in press a). The central finding from the second interview was that only the older group, who averaged 4½-years of age at the time of the fire alarm, showed convincing evidence of long-term memory for the event. None of the younger group were able to produce detailed memories, whereas some of the older group described detailed FM-like memories or were able to answer correctly direct questions about location, activity, etc. Pillemer et al. (in press a) provide the following example of an intact memory for the second interview:

> Well, it was popcorn, and it caught on fire, I guess. And I was stapling something. And I think I was the last one out, because I wouldn't leave until I stapled it … And I remember they were pulling me out, because, uh, that's pretty much it. And they figured out that it was, uh, umm, just the popcorn. And then we went back in. (Pillemer et al., in press a, p. 12)

The findings of Pillemer and his colleagues are very similar to those of Winograd and Killinger and lend further support to the view that there is some type of change between the ages of 4 and 5 years that leads to the emergence of FM-like memories. Moreover, other recent research also supports this view and Usher and Neisser (1993) found that adults' memories of personally significant events from childhood (birth of a sibling, death of a relative, etc.) increase with age at encoding (see also Sheingold & Tenney, 1982). Further compelling evidence of a developmental trend in the emergence of FMs was reported by Terr (1988) in a review of 20 children who had suffered childhood traumas when below the age of 5 years. The children in this study had experienced different types of traumas ranging from accidents through to repeated sexual abuse and all showed evidence of recalling their ordeals. However, only children who were over the age of about 36 months when the trauma had occurred were able to give detailed verbal accounts of the traumatic event or events. The children who had been below this age when their negative experiences occurred showed a wide range of behavioural evidence in their personalities and in their play indicating that they did indeed in some sense remember the event, but were unable to give full verbal accounts, although they could, occasionally, provide fragmentary details. Terr (1988) argues that younger children have unverbalisable "behavioural" memories for their traumas, whereas older children have vivid visual memories that support the generation of verbal accounts.

The ability to form FMs appears to emerge in childhood between the ages of 3 and 5 years and after this period the incidence of FMs to public events such as the assassination of JFK (Winograd & Killinger, 1983) and to emotional experiences (Terr, 1988; Usher & Neisser, 1993), rapidly increases with age. But are there also developmental changes in FM formation at the opposite end of the lifespan, in old age? As mentioned above, Yarmey and Bull (1978) found some evidence to suggest that subjects over the age of about 55 years had fewer FMs than younger subjects. In order to investigate this directly, Cohen, Conway, and Maylor (in press) contrasted the incidence of FMs for the resignation of the former British Prime Minister Margaret Thatcher in groups of older and younger subjects. [Note that Cohen and co-workers' (in press) study is a companion study to Conway et al. (in press), discussed in detail in Chapter 3, and uses exactly the same methodology.]

A group of 60 elderly subjects with a mean age of 71.6 years, all from professional backgrounds and most with university degrees, completed Conway and co-workers' (1994) FM questionnaire 10–14 days after the resignation and again approximately 1 year later. Two control groups were drawn from the subject samples used by Conway et al. One of these was a sample of 60 young UK subjects randomly selected from Conway and co-workers' study and the second was a group of 60 young US subjects also randomly selected from the same data set. A comparison between the responses from all three groups on the first questionnaire found no group differences and over 95% of all subjects provided memory descriptions and substantive answers to probe questions within 2 weeks of the event. Memory consistency scores were then calculated for the three groups using the procedure employed by Conway et al. The main finding was that significantly more of the young UK group had FMs (90%) than the elderly group (42%) and the young US group (29.8%).

Figure 4.6 shows the mean memory attribute accuracy scores for the young UK and elderly groups. For the young UK group, accuracy scores for all attributes were close to the maximum value of 2, indicating a high degree of consistency across the two questionnaires. In contrast, the elderly group show some consistency but only at a general rather than specific level and their scores were, on average, closer to 1 than 2. Note that in further comparisons, Cohen et al. (in press) found that the pattern of

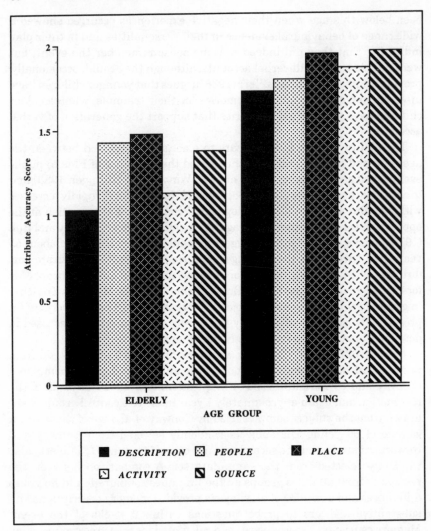

FIG. 4.6. Mean attribute accuracy scores for five canonical categories for elderly and young subjects (from Cohen et al., in press, fig. 2).

attribute accuracy scores was the same in the young US and elderly groups, suggesting that the memory deficits in the elderly group related more to aspects of forgetting than to other factors such as lifestyle. As roughly half the elderly subjects had FMs and half did not, it was possible to make further comparisons across these sub-groups and Fig. 4.7 shows the pattern of attribute accuracy scores for elderly subjects with and without FMs. The notable feature of Fig. 4.7 is that the elderly subjects who did not have FMs

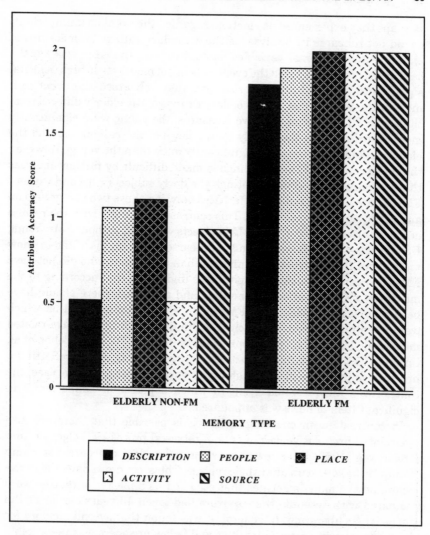

FIG. 4.7. Mean attribute accuracy scores for elderly subjects with and without FMs (from Cohen et al., in press, fig. 3).

showed a similar pattern of forgetting to the young US group. The elderly group should then have shown a high incidence of FMs comparable with that observed in the young UK group but they did not, and the frequency of FMs among the elderly was some 50% below that expected on the basis of the findings of Conway et al. (in press) with young UK subjects.

One possible reason for these findings is that the elderly did not respond to the news of the resignation in the same way as the younger subjects.

Perhaps they experienced no emotion, regarded the event as unimportant, or did not rehearse it. Analyses of the secondary ratings on measures of encoding and rehearsal variables found, however, that this was not the case. Elderly subjects rated the event as being of moderate to high personal significance, emotion and surprise, and they rehearsed the event to a moderate extent. In fact, the secondary ratings of the elderly differed from the young UK group on only two measures: the young were significantly more surprised than the elderly by the news of the resignation and the elderly talked about the news significantly more than the young. However, the interpretation of these findings is made difficult by further analyses that compared the secondary ratings of elderly subjects with and without FMs. There were no reliable differences between these two sub-groups on any of the secondary measures. This contrasts strikingly with the results of a comparison between young US subjects with and without FMs. Young US subjects with FMs were found to rehearse the event more and to know more about the Thatcher governments than their peers who did not have FMs. The general conclusion from these findings is that according to the measures of factors affecting encoding and rehearsal, there should have been a far higher incidence of FMs in the elderly group than that which was actually observed. As such, the findings indicate an age-related memory deficit emerging in people older than about 70 years. Cohen et al. (in press) argue that this is part of a larger memory deficit reflecting a progressive impairment in the ability to encode context. In this case, the context was the reception event in which a personally important and significant item of news was announced.

In contrast to an encoding deficit, it is possible that there are also age-related progressive decrements in retrieval processes. Wagenaar and Groeneweg (1990) interviewed survivors of a Nazi concentration camp (Camp Erika) 40 years after their release. The accounts of daily life in the camp and the many atrocities that occurred as a matter of routine were compared with accounts the survivors had given 40 years earlier at the time of their liberation. In general, it was found that overall memory for the camp, guards, various atrocities and fellow prisoners was remarkably accurate and detailed. However, some outstanding inconsistencies were also observed. For example, six of the survivors failed to recall accurately the names of guards who had tortured them or whom they had witnessed torture and murder others. Wagenaar and Groeneweg list a number of other striking discrepancies that clearly suggest the forgetting of important and central details in the context of otherwise good recall. Clearly, the extremely negative experiences of concentration camp prisoners should, at least according to the FMH, have given rise to remarkably vivid and durable FMs. But Wagenaar and Groeneweg's findings indicate that after a retention interval of 40+ years, these memories had become inconsistent. There are a number of competing explanations of these findings but a strong candidate account rests on the fact that many of the survivors were over the age of 70 years at the time of the second interview. In fact, Wagenaar and Groeneweg report some evidence that older survivors (in their 80s) had poorer memories than those who were younger (in their 60s). Flashbulb memories of extreme trauma may be unusually durable, but as an individual ages and the efficiency of memory processes declines, then even the most durable and vivid of memories may no longer be accessible and details may be lost or become inaccessible as memories start to fragment.

Finally, consider a study by Fitzgerald (1988) in which elderly subjects (mean age 68.7 years) recalled three highly vivid memories and for each memory completed a questionnaire modelled on the FM questionnaire developed by Rubin and Kozin (1984) and discussed earlier. Fitzgerald found a pattern of vivid memories very similar to that observed by Rubin and Kozin with the elderly group recalling few memories of public events and many memories of events high in personal significance. In an earlier study, Fitzgerald and Lawrence (1984) had sampled the autobiographical memories (rather than vivid memories specifically) of another group of elderly subjects (mean age 67.2 years) and this provided an opportunity to compare the patterns of vivid FM recall with the pattern of recall of autobiographical memories more generally.

Figure 4.8 shows the distributions of memories from different decades of life for vivid and autobiographical memories. Vivid or flashbulb memories were concentrated in the period when the subjects were 3–25 years of age, whereas autobiographical memories (not necessarily FM in nature) showed a very marked recency effect and most autobiographical memories were recalled from recent life periods (cf. Conway & Rubin, 1993, for a recent review of lifespan distributions of autobiographical memories, and Cohen & Faulkner, 1987, for an independently conducted study that essentially replicates Fitzgerald's findings). Fitzgerald (1988) proposed that this concentration of FMs relating to the period of childhood, adolescence and early adulthood reflects the emergence of a stable and integrated self (Erikson, 1978), in which events critical to the emerging self are elaboratively encoded.

However, as Neisser (1988) points out, only about one-third of the FMs collected by Fitzgerald (1988) could be classified as referring to critical life events such as births, deaths, marriages, etc. Many of the memories referred to first-time experiences (Robinson, 1992) and accidents which did not appear to be particularly critical points of change. Moreover, a large group of the FMs could not be classified and these, presumably, were of events of importance to the individual rememberer only. Thus, the formation of a stable self in late adolescence may play a role in the

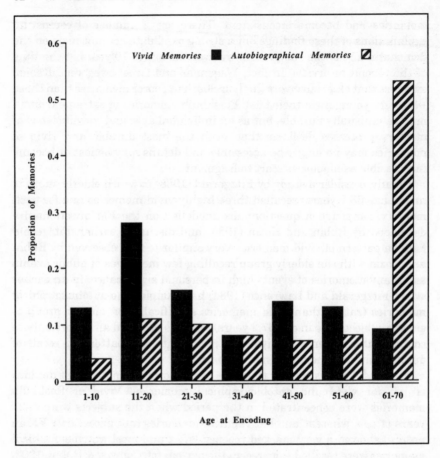

FIG. 4.8. Proportion of vivid memories and other autobiographical memories across the lifespan (data from Fitzgerald, 1988, table 1).

elaborative encoding of self-relevant events, but other events, not easily associated with the emergence of identity, can also be vividly retained. This suggests that FMs across the lifespan may arise for a variety of different reasons, only some of which are related to identity formation.

CONCLUSIONS

The central claim of the FMH is that when events are surprising and entail personal consequences, then FMs are formed. Does the study of "real" FMs support this conjecture of the FMH? The answer would seem to be "not without qualifications". Surprise at the occurrence of an event does not appear to be particularly significant in the formation of a wide range of

FMs. Although other sources of surprise, such as surprise associated with details of an event and/or the outcome of an event, may play some role in promoting FM formation. But as the appropriate measures have not yet been taken, the issue remains open. Personal consequentiality or importance would seem to be more central in the formation of FMs, particularly in memory for traumatic events. Similarly, intensity of emotional experience at encoding was found to be associated with both the incidence and elaborateness of FMs. However, neither personal consequentiality/importance nor intensity of emotional experience were found to be associated with FMs in all studies, although in any given study one of these usually was reliably associated with FMs. Thus, there may be some set of variables which are reflected in the rather global measures of importance and emotion that do promote FM formation and this is considered further in Chapter 6. What of rehearsal? A number of studies have now found FMs which subjects claim they have never related to anyone and it would seem from this that overt rehearsal is not necessary for the formation of FMs. Nevertheless, measures of rehearsal have occasionally been found to be associated with FMs and, consequently, rehearsal may make some small but significant contribution to FMs, possibly in their maintenance.

Perhaps the most striking finding to emerge from this review of "real" FMs is the incidence of FMs following highly stressful and traumatic experiences. Memories resulting from unique, one-off, traumatic experiences are highly detailed, can be intrusive, the patient avoids cues that might lead to recollection, and the healing process involves the patient coming to terms with his or her memory and integrating it with his or her autobiographical memory more generally. The events that lead to this pathological recall of FMs are clearly among the most personally consequential and significant of all life events and are typically associated with intense emotional experiences. In this respect, these events and the remarkable memories to which they give rise are highly compatible with the FMH's emphasis on personal consequentiality as a key factor in the generation of FMs.

CHAPTER FIVE

The Neurobiology of Flashbulb Memories

Neuroscientists studying memory formation have long known that a single exposure or a few exposures to a negative event can, in laboratory-trained animals, lead to behaviour which is very difficult to extinguish and which even when apparently "forgotten" can suddenly re-emerge in some later task. LeDoux (1992) concludes that such memories arising from emotional conditioning are "indelible". Indeed, this and other types of *reinforcement* originally lead Livingston (1967b) to propose his account of brain structures involved in the formation of vivid and long-lasting memories of events of "biological" significance (see Chapter 1). There have, of course, been many advances in the neurology of memory since Livingston's initial proposals. Nevertheless, the suggestion that events may be encoded differently when processed through different structures in the brain remains somewhat controversial, although on balance current evidence would seem to favour at least the possibility of differential encoding. In this chapter, we will briefly consider neurological structures implicated in memory formation and neuronal changes that underlie encoding. The aim is to provide an outline sketch only of the brain systems that support memory and to indicate how these might be related to the FMH (for a more complete account of neuropsychology, see Kolb & Wishaw, 1990).

MEMORY "CIRCUITS"

"Now Print!"

In Chapter 1, we touched briefly on Livingston's (1967b) neuroanatomical model of FM formation—his "Now Print!" mechanism. It is, however, misleading to characterise this as a single "mechanism" or "device", and Livingston himself was clearly aware that theoretical constructs in psychology such as perception, attention, emotion, language, memory, and so forth, are mediated by complex circuits or pathways in the brain that typically encompass interactive activation from many different sites. "Now Print!" is, then, more appropriately conceived as a process than a mechanism and Livingston (1967b, p. 576) comments:

> The steps that are postulated to occur are as follows: (1) reticular recognition of novelty; (2) limbic discrimination of biological meaning for that individual at that moment; (3) limbic discharge into the reticular formation; (4) a diffusely projecting reticular formation discharge distributed throughout both hemispheres, a discharge conceived to be a "Now Print!" order for memory, and finally, (5) all recent brain events, all recent conduction activities will be "printed" to facilitate repetition of similar conduction patterns.

Livingston further proposed that the full "Now Print!" process was only executed in its entirety when an event was of some personal biological significance, that is, when it was reinforcing. When an event was not reinforcing, then steps (3) through (5) of the "Now Print!" process would not be triggered. This suggests the possibility that for most everyday events the full "Now Print!" process does not operate—after all, events of biological significance are, virtually by definition, comparatively infrequent (how infrequent remains an open question). By this view, mundane everyday experiences, such as what one had for lunch last Tuesday, the trip to the supermarket 3 weeks ago, or the drive to work Friday last week, will not be retained in any great detail, although in the short-term—minutes, hours, possibly a few days—such memories can be retrieved. In order to understand the brain structures involved in the retention of everyday events as well as the retention of exceptional, personally significant events, a fuller account of the structures in the limbic system is required.

Dual Route to Memory Formation

The limbic system comprises a set of subcortical structures that have long been known to be involved in memory, emotion and motivated or goal-directed behaviour in general. Structures within the limbic system include the hippocampus, amygdala, septum, mamillary bodies, olfactory bulbs, fornix, thalamus and hypothalamus (cf. Kolb & Wishaw, 1990), and these sites are interconnected with one another, with other subcortical sites and with the neocortex. The hippocampus and amygdala form part of the temporal lobes (a region of the limbic system) and in particular part of the medial temporal lobe memory system (Squire, 1992). However, neither the medial temporal lobe memory system nor other regions of the limbic system are thought to be the areas where long-term memories are actually stored. Rather, these circuits are considered to mediate, among other functions, the initial formation of memories with long-term storage taking place in other areas, such as neocortex or sites involved in sensory processing.

One of the main sources of knowledge about the role of limbic system circuits in memory encoding comes from studies of brain-damaged individuals. Amnesic patients show many different types of memory impairments and a common pattern of impairment is an inability to encode new experiences into long-term memory following brain injury with some preservation of memories encoded before the injury occurred (see Parkin & Leng, 1993, for a detailed account of the amnesic syndrome). Naturally occurring brain damage leading to amnesia (i.e. from strokes, head injuries and infections) often occurs at multiple sites in the limbic system and frontal lobes. Thus, if there is a memory circuit or circuits, then this is probably interrupted at a number of points in amnesic patients. However, amnesias have also been observed in patients who have undergone neurosurgery to excise a part of the brain identified as the locus of intractable epileptic fits. Undoubtedly, the most well-researched case is that of the patient H.M. (Scoville & Milner, 1957), whose epilepsy was cured following removal of both hippocampus and amygdala but who presented with a profound amnesia following his operation and was unable to encode new events into long-term memory (see Parkin & Leng, 1993; see also Conway, 1993, for an account of impairments of autobiographical memory in amnesic patients).

Mishkin and Appenzeller (1987), in reviewing a large body of work investigating the role of limbic system structures in memory and learning, observed that in animals the amnesic syndrome could not be induced by removal of the hippocampus or amygdala alone. Nevertheless, removal of either one of these structures caused some memory impairments in laboratory animals, as did the isolated removal of other limbic system structures such as the thalamus and hypothalamus (see Mishkin & Appenzeller, 1987, p. 68). The particular pattern of impairments associated with disruptions to different limbic system circuits gave rise to the formation of a dual-route model of memory encoding focused on circuits associated with the hippocampus and amygdala (Mishkin, 1982; Mishkin & Appenzeller, 1987; for reviews of similar proposals, see Mayes, 1988; Parkin, 1987) and this model is shown in Fig. 5.1.

Evidence from human amnesics tends to fit this model, although there remain some patients whose brain injury and resulting amnesia do not fit specific predictions of the dual-route model (Parkin & Leng, 1993, pp. 132–134). In terms of the FMH, one of the key questions is whether these different circuits contribute selectively to the formation of different types of memory. In particular, could it be the case that one of these circuits is specialised for the encoding of highly vivid, durable FMs? Research into the different functions of the hippocampus and amygdala suggest that could be the case.

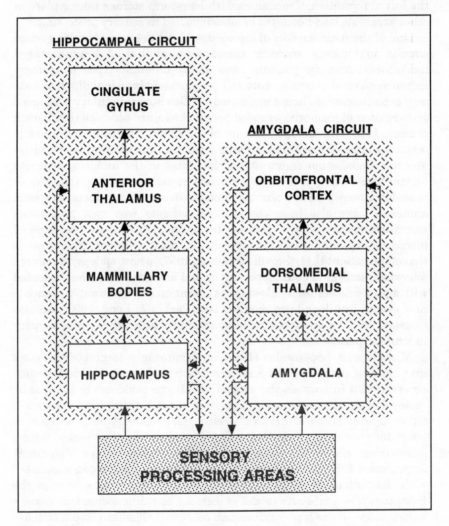

FIG. 5.1. Dual routes to memory formation (after Mishkin & Appenzeller, 1987).

The Hippocampus

One of the most comprehensive of current reviews of the role of the hippocampal formation in memory is given in Squire (1992), where a wide range of evidence from studies of the human amnesic syndrome and animal models of this syndrome (using monkeys and rats) is considered. The evidence from magnetic resonance studies of living individuals, surgical intervention studies with humans and animals, and post-mortem studies, converges on the view that the hippocampus and surrounding regions connecting to neocortex are critically involved in memory formation. The case is also made that the amygdala does not contribute directly to memory formation and this is because in many previous studies where the amygdala had been damaged or removed, so had other critical regions (perirhinal and parahippocampal cortices) connecting the hippocampus to neocortical areas. Squire reports that monkeys with amygdala damage only exhibit emotional disturbances but no impairments of memory. In contrast, monkeys with hippocampal damage and damage to associated cortex show marked memory impairments but no abnormal emotional behaviour. Thus the case is made that the hippocampus and closely related structures are the critical sites in memory formation.

The evidence suggests that the effects of the hippocampus are in the formation of a "simple memory, a summary sketch, a gross trace, an index, a device for constructing unique configurations among stimuli, or for collating widely stored pieces of experience" (Squire, 1992, p. 208). Thus, the hippocampus binds together sources of processing occurring in other brain areas (sensory and neocortical areas) to create a structure that can index, presumably, original processing undertaken at encoding. It is also proposed that the hippocampus may play some role in the retrieval of a memory when a cue is again processed through the system and activates the outline sketch or index formed at some earlier time. But these effects of the hippocampal system are temporary and over some comparatively short period of time (hours or days) it is thought that slow-acting processes in neocortex take over and the memory is consolidated in long-term memory at sites outside the hippocampal system. It is possible that such consolidation is mediated by connections between the hippocampus and neocortex. This view of the mnemonic functions of the hippocampus has particular relevance to the FMH, as it clearly supports the notion that some memories, possibly of mundane everyday events, may not be consolidated in neocortical sites. Such memories might exist temporarily in "outline" form in the hippocampus and associated structures for some limited period of time until they are "forgotten". The way in which memories are forgotten is unknown, but one possibility is that the assembly of neurons that represent a hippocampal memory are subsequently used to represent other memories and in this way the original memory is gradually "overwritten". When no further record exists in other brain areas, an overwritten memory is permanently lost.

The Amygdala

Despite Squire's (1992) arguments that the amygdala plays no direct role in memory formation, there is an extensive literature demonstrating just the opposite—that the amygdala is a critical brain structure in memory formation and especially in the formation of emotionally toned memories. McGaugh and his colleagues (for reviews, see McGaugh, 1991; 1992; McGaugh et al., 1989) have investigated the mediating influence of the amygdala in the formation of memories for events featuring aversive stimuli. In these studies, naturally occurring memory-modulating hormones and drugs associated with stressful and negative events are first identified and then used to alter memory, either by enhancing or inhibiting memory consolidation. The effects of these substances (e.g. adrenal epinephrine, etc., and their agonists and antagonists) are typically examined in post-training studies. In this type of procedure, an animal first learns a task (often an avoidance task) and shortly after acquisition is treated with one of the hormones. Retention of the task can be enhanced or inhibited in a critical period after acquisition according to the particular stress-related hormone or drug administered and according to dosage. However, after some period of time, these treatments have no influence upon memory, suggesting that their effect in the initial period shortly after acquisition is upon memory consolidation. Indeed, treatment with a stress-related hormone thought to enhance memory for naturally occurring aversive events can enhance memory (when administered in the post-training period) even for emotionally neutral events. McGaugh (1992) concludes that several neuromodulatory systems come together and interact in the amygdala and the effects of hormones and drugs upon the amygdala is to enhance or inhibit memory consolidation by stimulating these systems. As with the hippocampus, the evidence suggests that memories are only temporarily held at this site and, presumably, long-term storage takes place elsewhere, perhaps via pathways from the amygdala to other brain areas. Unlike the hippocampus, then, the memory effects of the amygdala appear to be initiated by emotional experiences and by the release of hormones associated with (negative) affect and stress.

The amygdala may play an even more central role in emotional experience than simply mediating the formation of emotional memories. The amygdala receives inputs from both sensory processing areas in the neocortex and thalamus and it projects to brainstem regions that mediate behavioural and autonomic responses. Thus, LeDoux (1992) argues that the amygdala is well placed to modulate sensory processing into emotional processing and to regulate subsequent emotional experience. Indeed, LeDoux (1992) proposes that the amygdala is the brain structure that initiates emotional experience [previous commentators have more usually identified the hypothalamus (a limbic system structure interconnected to the amygdala) as the generator of emotional experience]. Some evidence for this view comes from studies of the Kluver–Bucy syndrome (Kluver & Bucy, 1937), in which lesions of the temporal lobe were found to lead to bizarre behaviours. For instance, monkeys with such lesions attempted to copulate with the same sex, with animals from other species, and apparently lost fear responses to previously aversive objects. In general, the animals no longer responded to objects in appropriate ways. Later research found the Kluver–Bucy syndrome to be associated with lesions to the amygdala alone and more recent research has now extensively implicated the amygdala in other aspects of emotional experience (cf. LeDoux, 1992, for a review).

LeDoux (1992) focused on the thalamo-amygdala and the cortico-amygdala pathways. The thalamo-amygdala pathway facilitates access by the amygdala to very early stages of sensory processing at a point when the sensory processing cycle has yet to result in anything like a complete representation of an event or even of whole objects featuring in an event. This pathway is shorter than the cortico-amygdala pathway and so allows fast access to very early stages in the processing of an event. In contrast, the cortico-amygdala connection, which is longer and therefore slower, supports amygdala processing at later stages of sensory processing cycles when an event and its objects and actions have been more completely represented. Emotional processing supported by the amygdala can then influence both very early stages of sensory processing and later stages—perhaps an emotional response incorrectly initiated earlier in processing can be terminated or modulated in some other way by the involvement of the cortico-amygdala route or, on the other hand, an emotional response initiated by early processes might subsequently be amplified by late processing via the cortico-amygdala circuit.

LeDoux (1992) cautiously concludes that there may be several distinct brain circuits that support the encoding of different types of memories. The hippocampal circuit mediates the encoding of non-emotional declarative memories (cf. Squire, 1992) that represent factual knowledge and knowledge about events low in hedonic tone. The amygdala circuit codes for memories of highly emotional events, often with a negative valence. Yet other circuits, not considered here, may support the encoding of habits, procedural knowledge and other types of learning.

Other Brain Areas Involved in Memory

The strong concentration of research on the medial temporal lobe memory system has tended to distract research attention from other structures clearly and centrally involved in the formation of memories. For example, the thalamus and hypothalamus, two large brain structures of the diencephalon adjacent to the temporal lobes and beneath the cerebral cortex, are known to feature in memory. In particular, amnesic patients with Wernicke–Korsakoff syndrome often have lesions of the dorso-medial thalamic nucleus and the mamillary bodies (see Parkin & Leng, 1993, Chapter 3; and Fig. 5.1). Korsakoff patients typically have a marked anterograde amnesia and so cannot encode new events and, additionally, often have a temporally graded retrograde amnesia such that events occurring before the onset of the chronic phase of the illness are not recalled but events from childhood and early adolescence are recalled, often at levels comparable to non-brain-damaged control subjects. Currently, the functions of these diencephalic structures in memory formation are not known, although it is to be expected, given their prominence in the aetiology of Wernicke–Korsakoff syndrome, that they will be found to make critical contributions to encoding. These contributions may feature the relay of information to the medial temporal lobe memory system, which in turn may influence the nature of encoding undertaken by the hippocampus and amygdala.

One of the more recent and fascinating developments in studies of amnesia is the discovery that injury to the frontal lobes can also give rise to memory disorders (cf. Baddeley & Wilson, 1986; Parkin & Leng, 1993; Shallice, 1988; Stuss & Benson, 1984). Indeed, many amnesics, particularly Wernicke–Korsakoff patients, have damage to these areas as well as lesions of limbic system structures. The type of amnesia associated with damage to the frontal lobes does not necessarily involve an inability to access knowledge in long-term memory, nor is it associated with an impairment in the encoding of new information. Rather, frontal lobe amnesics show an impairment in fully retrieving autobiographical memories, what Baddeley and Wilson (1986) called a "clouding" of memory, and/or confabulations are present. Confabulations in these patients typically take the form of reports of events that did not in fact occur (Baddeley & Wilson, 1986; Parkin & Leng, 1993; Shallice, 1988). However, it is most intriguing that such confabulations feature actors, actions and objects that are from the rememberer's past and are often presented in the form of a narrative in which the described events could, plausibly, have actually happened. (Although it should be noted that other types of confabulations may take the form of fantastic or implausible accounts of past events which the patient clearly could not have experienced.) It would appear, then, that the frontal lobes are critically involved in memory retrieval (Conway, 1993; Shallice, 1988).

The amygdala projects directly to regions of the frontal system (see Fig. 5.1) and it seems possible that by this route the frontal system may also be able to influence memory encoding directly, at least when this involves the amygdala. The frontal lobes mediate many different cognitive functions, including central control processes and aspects of personality (cf. Shallice, 1988). Norman and Shallice (1980; see also Baddeley, 1986; Conway, in press; Shallice, 1988) propose that the frontal lobes support the operation of a central supervisory attentional system (SAS) and that one of the functions of this system is in coordinating activation in, and output from, long-term memory. The suggestion here is that in addition to this the SAS may also coordinate memory encoding, and its most direct influence may be present when the to-be-encoded event features emotional experience. I will return to this point below and later in Chapter 6.

MEMORY "MECHANISMS"

Current evidence implicates a number of limbic system structures in memory encoding and these form circuits in which cascades of information relating to current experience are processed into memories. Important though these structures are to memory formation, there most also be some specific, biological way in which the brain changes when a memory is formed. Recently, a general mechanism of neuronal plasticity has been identified and sites in which this plasticity is known to take place are the hippocampus and amygdala.

Long-term Potentiation

Brain plasticity in response to stimulation has been identified at the neuronal level in the brain and takes place at the synapses. Bliss and Lomo (1973) discovered the process of long-term potentiation (LTP) when studying cells in the rabbit hippocampus. In LTP, the excitatory post-synaptic potential is strengthened and remains strengthened for a period of hours. One way in which LTP is thought to occur is by the release of the excitatory amino acid (EAA) glutamate. There are a number of EAA receptors, two of which are the AMPA (amino methylisoxazole propionic acid) and NMDA (N-methyl-D-aspartate) receptors. AMPA receptors in response to increases in glutamate rapidly depolarise, whereas NMDA depolarise more slowly and remain depolarised for a longer period of time. Importantly, these two sets of EAA receptors interact so that depolarisation of AMPA receptors allows depolarisation of NMDA receptors and it is this interaction which leads to the trans-synaptic neuronal changes that facilitate subsequent transmissions. Moreover, other associated synapses of the neuron, although only weakly activated, may also show LTP. In this way, the LTP process supports the rapid and long-lasting learning of associated signals (see Brown, Chapman, Kairiss, & Keenan, 1988, for a review).

LTP in the Hippocampus and Amygdala

Long-term potentiation has been identified in a number of circuits within the hippocampus and it seems likely that this is indeed a site of neural plasticity in which memory formation could take place. LeDoux (1992) and McGaugh (1992) discuss the role of NMDA-LTP in the amygdala for which there is, as yet, no direct evidence. However, the thalamo-amygdala pathway utilises glutamate in synaptic transmissions and NMDA receptors are located in the region of the amygdala connecting to the thalamus. Moreover, blockage of NMDA receptors in the amygdala prevents the formation of emotional memories (LeDoux, 1992), all of which strongly suggests that NMDA-LTP may well take place in the amygdala and areas associated with it. Thus, both the hippocampus and amygdala utilise the LTP mechanism and, therefore, may be sites of (temporary) memory storage.

Glucose and Memory

A more general memory mechanism of memory formation has recently been suggested by Gold (1992), who noted that despite the effects of adrenalin (a hormone associated with stressful experiences) in enhancing post-training retention of a variety of aversively reinforced tasks, this hormone does not itself cross the blood–brain barrier to influence brain processes directly. Instead, it transpires that the effects of adrenalin are in promoting the levels of circulating glucose within the brain. As Gold (1992) points out, glucose is also known to enhance memory when administered in the critical post-training phase and, as we have already seen, glucose and substances closely related to it play a central role in the LTP memory mechanism. Interestingly, Gold (1992) reported that these effects of glucose on memory may be attenuated in old age and experiments in which glucose was administered to elderly individuals taking various memory tests found an enhancement of memory. In connection with this, it is perhaps worth noting Cohen and co-workers' (in press) finding of a significantly lower than expected frequency of FMs among elderly subjects (see Chapter 4), even though ratings of importance and affect were at appropriate levels for FM formation. If Gold's glucose model of memory formation is correct, then Cohen and co-workers' findings may have been mediated by an age-related deficiency in brain glucose levels.

Gold (1992) speculates that when a negative emotional event occurs, then this triggers the release of hormones that act to raise glucose levels and the increase in glucose enhances both memory and other aspects of cognition. According to Gold, the effect of glucose upon memory is in the form of an inverted-U, such that very low levels do not support memory encoding and neither do chronically high levels. Normal levels of circulating glucose support the encoding of everyday memories and, possibly, when the amount of glucose rises to some optimal level, then FMs are formed. By this admittedly speculative view FMs are, then, a special case of the "normal" encoding of memories.

CONCLUSIONS: ROUTES TO MEMORY FORMATION

In everyday experience, events differ in their personal impact—many are mundane and routine, others impinge directly on personal plans and goals, yet others may entail intense stress and/or affect. It clearly makes adaptive sense that memory should have evolved to represent this fluctuating state of affairs in experience with some events being retained in detail for long periods of time, whereas others are rapidly lost or not processed into long-term storage in the first place. The evidence briefly reviewed in this chapter suggests two possibilities.

The first possibility is that there is a general encoding process, possibly centred on the hippocampus and the influence of circulating levels of glucose upon the LTP memory process. Mundane and routine everyday experiences do not lead to the release of hormones that increase glucose levels and so the outline "sketch" memories represented by the hippocampus do not receive any special encoding. When an experience promotes the release of the appropriate hormones, then LTP circuits in the hippocampus respond to raised glucose levels and a memory is consolidated in long-term memory more efficiently—perhaps making that memory more detailed, durable and accessible than memories encoded under normal levels of circulating glucose.

The second possibility is that the effect of the release of hormones associated with affect is more selective. The neurochemical systems associated in the amygdala may interact in the presence of increased glucose levels and in this way lead to the formation of FMs. This second possibility has a number of attractions from a psychological point of view, as memory formation via the amygdala facilitates the involvement of cognitive control processes associated with the frontal lobe regions. Emotions are undoubtedly complex cognitive events (see Chapter 6), and although they may be mediated by limbic system structures, they must also be modulated by central control processes. Moreover, by no means all emotional experiences are personally significant and, therefore, although emotion may be important in the formation of FMs, so must other factors. Thus, a brain structure known to be involved in emotion and emotional memories that is also influenced by other brain areas involved in control processes provides a promising model for the effects of emotion upon memory. We will return to this suggestion in Chapter 6.

Finally, a further option, not considered earlier, is that as memories are multi-attribute knowledge structures (see Conway, in press; Dewhurst & Conway, in press; Johnson, Hastroudi, & Lindsay, 1993), then they may be represented in terms of their attributes and distributed across many brain subsystems. Kesner (1991) has developed a neuroanatomical model that attempts to capture this multi-attribute aspect of autobiographical memories and Fig. 5.2 is a much simplified version of his model. In fact, in Kesner's model there are two broad sets of brain processing structures. One set is characterised as a data-based memory system and this is shown in Fig. 5.2. The data-based memory system is essentially concerned with creating a representation of an event in long-term memory and structures within this system process and code different attributes of an event. Not shown in Fig. 5.2 are structures in the expectancy-based memory system that are concerned with prior knowledge and which can be used independently of event encoding (for further details, see Kesner, 1991, fig. 13.1). From the perspective of the FMH, one advantage of Kesner's approach is that multi-attribute memories can be created in which the level of detail and centrality of any single attribute to the whole memory can vary. Thus, multi-attribute memories for events low in personal significance and emotion (everyday memories) will have relatively reduced representations for processing occurring in the amygdala and, perhaps, the caudate (see Fig. 5.2). Flashbulb memories, on the other hand, will have representations from these and other structures in the data-based memory system. Conceivably, it is this more complete range of representation in data-based processing subsystems that confers clarity and durability upon FMs. The clarity arises because, quite simply, more information is retained, and the durability occurs because a more elaborate cognitive "map" of processing in the many different subsystems must be created for these types of memories. The elaborate map or trace of the processing is less vulnerable to the effects of decay and interference than the less elaborate maps associated with events where subsystem processing is, by comparison, attenuated. Thus, rather than just dual routes to memory encoding there may be multiple routes, and the creation of FMs occurs when all or the majority of data-based processing subsystems are engaged.

Overall, it seems reasonable to conclude that Livingston's (1967b) original model was remarkably prescient. Subsequent research has supported the general framework of his model, in that it now appears that

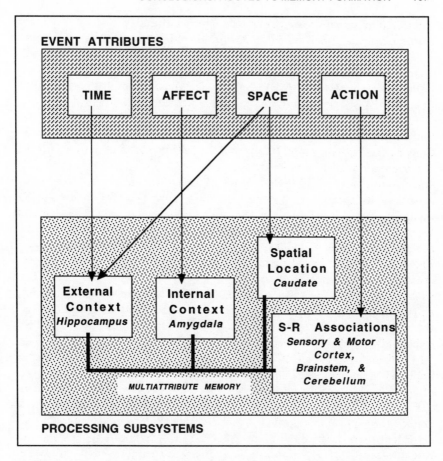

FIG. 5.2. Multi-attribute memories and processing subsystems (after Kesner, 1991, fig. 13.1).

there may be limbic system brain processes that mediate the differential encoding of events, although the specific reticular activation component of the "Now Print!" process does not appear to have received much support in subsequent research. Nevertheless, the current evidence converges on the view that the encoding of emotional events differs from the encoding of non-emotional events or events low in emotion. The FMH proposes privileged encoding of FMs compared with other types of memories and the findings reviewed here lend at least provisional support to this conjecture.

CHAPTER SIX

Revising the Flashbulb
Memory Hypothesis

The evidence for the existence of highly detailed, vivid and durable memories, FMs, is both extensive and compelling. The studies reviewed in Chapter 3 found FMs to be basically accurate and the findings considered in Chapter 4 strongly implicated the role of affect in the formation of FMs. Other findings, however, identified personal importance as the more critical factor in FM encoding. In contrast, rehearsal was rarely found to be associated with FMs. Moreover, a review of neuropsychological research suggested that there may, indeed, be isolatable brain processes that mediate the encoding of emotional memories. On balance, then, the findings would appear to favour, in broad outline, Brown and Kulik's (1977) model of FM formation—the flashbulb memory hypothesis (FMH) outlined in Chapter 1. Nevertheless, and despite this body of evidence, the FMH suffers from a number of shortcomings, the most pressing of which is the high level of generality of central theoretical concepts such as "personal consequentiality" and "emotion". Also, the proposed function of FMs, to preserve knowledge of events of biological significance, appears rather limited as an account of the full range of FMs considered in the preceding chapters. In this final chapter, FMH concepts are linked to recent theoretical developments and the wider functions of FMs are explored. But first I turn to a general account of the nature of FMs and their correlates.

WHAT ARE FLASHBULB MEMORIES?

In Brown and Kulik's original paper, FMs were characterised as detailed and durable memories that contained specific knowledge (location, others, activities, affect and informant) of an event in which surprising and consequential news was first learned. In general, some variation of these categories of information are retained across all FMs. For events which do not feature items of news, then obviously categories such as "informant" are not present (although "perpetrator" might be; see Chapter 4). Also present are idiosyncratic details relating to the reception event and these are often vivid, highly specific and apparently retained almost at random. These idiosyncratic features may facilitate the phenomenological experience of the "live" quality of FMs, in which an event is almost relived rather than simply remembered. Certainly something like this would appear to be the case for memories of traumatic events that originally involved intense emotions (Brewin et al., 1993; Terr, 1988).

But is this pattern of memory content unique to FMs or do all autobiographical memories retain knowledge of the "canonical" categories? In a series of experiments, Anderson and Conway (1993) found that subjects who recalled autobiographical memories to a wide range of verbal cues were able to provide information on most of the canonical categories for most of their memories, even though this information was not directly requested. But highly specific recall of minutiae was not present in these memories and was rarely observed in subsequent studies that probed directly for this type of detail (Anderson, 1993). Thus, one conclusion is that FMs are a special type of autobiographical memory which preserve in fine-grain the details of an event; and this fits well with McCloskey and co-workers' (1988) proposal that FMs are simply "ordinary" memories retained to some unusually high standard of clarity.

However, the claim that FMs are simply high-resolution autobiographical memories may gloss over other important differences between the two types of memory. According to one account (Anderson & Conway, 1993; Barsalou, 1988; Conway, 1992; in press; Conway & Rubin, 1993), most autobiographical memories are temporary, dynamic and hence unstable mental representations. By this view, cyclic retrieval processes, initiated and modulated by central control processes, probe complex multi-layered autobiographical knowledge structures in long-term memory. A memory is "retrieved" once a stable pattern of activation is established across long-term memory knowledge structures. Patterns of activation in long-term memory are determined by the particular knowledge used to probe memory, by the "route" followed through accessed knowledge structures, and by the requirements of the current task. It follows from this view that "memories" are temporary patterns of activation that require effortful maintenance and which are inherently unstable both in the short term and in the long term over repeated retrievals of the same memory (Conway & Anderson, 1993; Conway, in press). The main thrust of this view of autobiographical memory is that memories are *constructed* from different types of autobiographical knowledge rather than, for instance, directly accessed in the form of some "holistic", discrete and integrated memory "unit". Memory construction is constrained by the organisation of different types of autobiographical knowledge that "channel" activation in particular directions within the autobiographical knowledge base by limiting the cues available to access one region from another (see Conway, 1992; in press).

One feature of this constructivist model of autobiographical memory is that the organisation of knowledge of specific events varies in its coherence. For many memories, organisation will be comparatively "loose" and construction will be effortful. In this case, retrieval of specific details may be difficult or even impossible and knowledge retrieved for the same memory on different occasions will change with, and be highly sensitive to, task demands and cues that become available during the retrieval episode. In contrast, the organisation of knowledge for other memories may be much tighter, integrated and coherent. When organisation is tight or coherent, memories can be retrieved as "whole" units and constructive processes are primarily limited to the access phase of retrieval. Consider, then, a large and complex knowledge base—the autobiographical knowledge base—in which different types of autobiographical knowledge are organised to varying degrees and which is highly sensitive to cues. Regions of this knowledge base may contain dense areas in which knowledge is integrated to form, as it were, "whole" units. Such densely organised regions might be thought of as "local minima" in the autobiographical memory landscape. When one of these regions is contacted by activation channelled from associated knowledge structures, then the activation becomes confined to that region and the knowledge represented there becomes immediately and fully available to the centrally controlled retrieval processes. At this point, control processes must actively intervene to redirect the retrieval process if the accessed knowledge is discrepant with current task demands.

What types of knowledge might be represented in this integrated and coherent fashion? There are a number of possible candidates. For instance, expertise in a knowledge domain may lead to integrated organisation of knowledge (Anderson, 1987)—most people are experts on their own family, their career and other domains arising from personal interests (i.e. a particular type of literature, a sport or particular team, hobby or pastime). Similarly, often repeated events may lead to the formation of personal scripts that form dense regions in autobiographical memory. Linton (1982) describes how her own autobiographical memory for professional meetings gradually transformed into a script-like representation about professional meetings in general (see Conway, 1990, for related findings). However, the suggestion here is that FMs constitute the prototypic case of tightly organised, dense regions of the autobiographical knowledge base and, therefore, FMs differ from "ordinary" autobiographical memories not just in the specificity of the knowledge they contain but also in the way in which that knowledge is organised and accessed in long-term memory.

Flashbulb memories are unusually detailed, clear and tightly organised memories, and once accessed in long-term memory their contents become fully available. Brown and Kulik (1977) proposed that FMs consist of a "core" non-verbal, image-based representation, from which FM accounts can be derived. According to the FMH, this "core" representation is highly durable and immune to change. The findings from studies of emotional memories, particularly those involving intense and negative affect associated with stress-related conditions such as PTSD (see Chapter 4), do appear to take this form. Intrusive and repetitively recalled memories of trauma primarily feature images, sensations and feelings from the original event (Terr, 1988; Walker, 1992). This notion of a "core" memory from which many different (verbal) accounts can be derived is compatible with views of autobiographical memory more generally. Anderson and Conway (1993) distinguished between the organisation and content of autobiographical memory and processing or "editing" directed at retrieved knowledge. A task may require, for instance, relating a humorous story, a strategic self-disclosure or some other presentational constraint, and these task demands will impose constraints on how a search of memory is initiated and directed, and on how outputs from memory are evaluated and edited into the appropriate narrative from. Thus, all autobiographical memories, not just FMs, might be considered to have a "core" that is separate from a verbal account. The difference is that for the majority of autobiographical memories, the "core" is a temporary pattern of activation across some delimited set of autobiographical memory knowledge structures, whereas for FMs the core is an integrated, densely organised region of the autobiographical knowledge base.

The durability and consistency of FMs further distinguishes them from most autobiographical memories. However, Brown and Kulik's claim that the "core" representation is immune to change is questionable. The concentration camp survivors in Wagenaar and Groeneweg's (1990) study misidentified crucial features of their experience, Terr's (1988) post-trauma children occasionally added information to their memory accounts, and the witnesses in Yuille and Cutshall's (1986) study were mistaken on at least some details (see Chapter 4). Despite these findings, there are a number of lines of argument that can be used to defend the "immutable core" idea. Flashbulb memories may be unchanging until the cognitive system itself changes (i.e. in development and ageing). As FMs are incomplete records of events, then some inferences are to be expected, but this does not mean that the core representation has changed. Finally, to the extent that FMs are records of a person's interpretation of an event, then they can be at variance with objective fact, yet this does not mean that the core representation has changed. The key issue would seem to be the remarkable consistency of FMs, rather than issues of accuracy *per se*, and the fact that FMs are in the main so consistent over long periods of time certainly suggests that they are resistant to change or at least more resistant than most memories.

Nonetheless, a problem remains and that is how to account for findings demonstrating that FMs sustain an impressive level of consistency over long retention intervals and *at the same time* show the introduction of new information. According to the model of integrated organisation developed here, FMs can be modified while at the same time original core representations, formed at encoding, remain unchanged. For example, new types of organisation may be added to the original core representation. As many different narratives are generated from a core, it is only to be expected that some record of these will also be represented in long-term memory, almost certainly along with the core representation. The core may remain unchanged in its own organisation and content, but as other knowledge is represented in close association with the core, then the organisation of autobiographical knowledge at that point in the knowledge base will change. On the other hand, there may be active and direct attempts to change the core representation—as in the therapeutic treatment of patients who have suffered trauma. Often the aim of therapy is to reduce the strong emotion associated with the FM and to alter the interpretation placed upon the memory. As therapy is frequently effective, it can only be assumed that the FM has been changed in some way. Again this may occur not by changes to the densely integrated organisation of the FM itself, but more by changes to knowledge closely associated with the core representation such that the core is added to or extended in some way as the new interpretation becomes linked to the core.

That FMs of trauma remain vivid but become less disturbing would seem to lend some support to the view that FMs are not resistant to change but at the same time remain stable. Terr (1988) describes a number of cases in which verbal additions were added to memories of trauma, although the memories themselves remained consistent and unchanging. The case of a young boy who had been kidnapped provides a good example:

> A 39-month-old boy, Alan, had been kidnapped for ransom by a stranger. At first he had blamed his mother because she had given him up at gunpoint, but by age 5 or 6 he exchanged fears—the fear of separation for a newly

developed fear of death. Alan, at age 8, had already given two complete, accurate versions of the kidnapping when he commented, "I already know what it's like to die—to be killed. I learned that when I was 5 or 6 years old. I realize now that the man who took me could have killed me. But I think back now on when I was 3 and kidnapped ... I used to blame Mom for letting him have me. I thought she shouldn't have given me up. But I now know that he had a gun on Mom and he would've killed her. Now I feel better about Mom, but a little worse about me". (Terr, 1988, p. 102)

Thus, FMs, initially encoded as tightly organised, coherent representations, may be added to by further experiences. The new representations which are formed need not change in any way the original FM, but as they are created an original FM becomes part of a more extensive system of knowledge and when accessed is accessed through this system. Perhaps it is in this way that the interpretation placed on a FM and the emotion attached to it can be altered over time, by the modulating influence of new knowledge structures constructed around the FM.

In summary, the evidence indicates that FMs are more detailed and vivid than most autobiographical memories. The constructive account of autobiographical memory suggests that the knowledge represented in a FM may be more integrated and "holistic" in character than most autobiographical memories which appear to have a distributed type of representation. Flashbulb memories do apparently survive in consistent form over long retention intervals, and this may be because of their integrated and coherent organisation. There are, however, few reasons to accept the claim that FMs are unchanging. The evidence from survivors of trauma is that FMs can change (Chapter 4), particularly in their interpretation and in the emotion they engender when retrieved. The constructivist view of autobiographical memory suggests how the content of FMs might be preserved but yet alter their meaning.

WHAT ARE THE CONDITIONS FOR FLASHBULB MEMORY FORMATION?

The FMH emphasises surprise and personal consequentiality as the key factors in triggering brain events that lead to FM formation. But the findings do not lend unequivocal support to this aspect of the FMH. The problem here, however, hinges not so much on the actual findings but more on what ratings—such as surprise, consequentiality, importance and emotion—measure. In particular, do these ratings all measure a common construct but to different degrees? That is to say, do all these measures share common variance and also have unique variance? Figure 6.1 depicts one way in which these variables might have unique variance, be

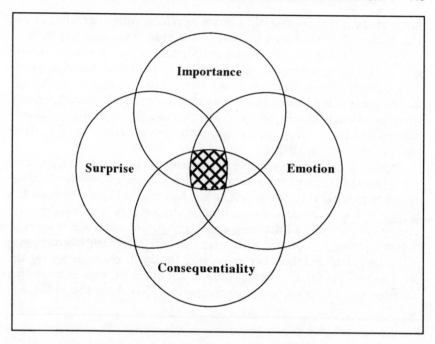

FIG. 6.1. Ideal interrelations of four variables predicting FM formation.

associated with one another, and all load on a common factor (the hatched area in Fig. 6.1). According to Fig. 6.1, FMs would be formed when an event fell within the central hatched area where surprise, consequentiality, importance and emotion overlap. Clearly, however, this cannot be wholly correct, and in Chapter 4 we saw that events can lead to FMs even when the occurrence of those events is not surprising. (Although, of course, aspects other than the occurrence of an event may lead to the experience of surprise; see Chapter 4.) Furthermore, the findings reviewed in Chapters 3 and 4 clearly demonstrate that personal consequentiality, importance and emotion are strongly associated with the emergence of FMs. Thus, the relationship between these three factors is almost certainly closer than that depicted in Fig. 6.1. But personal consequentiality, importance and emotion may have unique variance also. For example, an event may feature intense emotion but be of little or no personal consequentiality and importance—as writers, movie-makers and other entertainers have long known. Yet, it seems unlikely that an event could be high in personal importance and entail no personal consequences or emotion. Against this suggestion is Rubin and Kozin's (1984; see Chapter 4) finding that personally important events, which had given rise to FMs, were not reliably associated with consequentiality. But one problem with this finding is that the student subjects who took part in the study may have experienced difficulty in using the consequentiality rating scale—certainly similar groups of subjects in Conway and co-workers' (1994) study found this scale very difficult to use and for this reason the scale was dropped from Conway and co-workers' FM questionnaire. In short, it seems possible that personal consequentiality, importance and emotion would generally be closely interrelated in everyday experience, with surprise also related to these three to at least some degree.

Figure 6.2 depicts the possible relationship between surprise, personal consequentiality, importance and emotion suggested by the findings reviewed in the earlier chapters. The hatched area in Fig. 6.2 represents a region where personal consequentiality, importance and emotion are closely interrelated and the lined area highlights a region where surprise becomes strongly associated with these three factors. Flashbulb memories will arise in either of these two areas, with the lined area representing the ideal conditions for FM formation and the hatched area representing conditions very favourable to the emergence of FMs. According to Fig. 6.2,

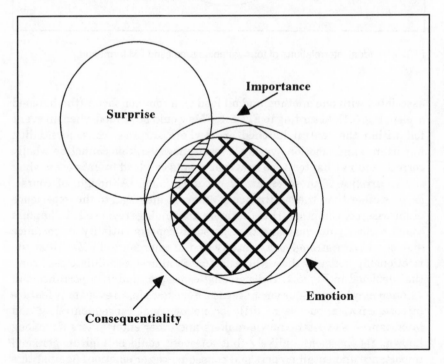

FIG. 6.2. Probable interrelations of four variables predicting FM formation.

when an event is surprising, personally consequential, important and emotional, the probability of FM formation is maximised. When an event is not surprising (at least in its probability of occurrence) but is still personally consequential, important and emotional, the probability of FMs being formed remains high, although it is not at a maximum. Conway and co-workers' (1994) findings indicate that importance is the critical factor that interacts with emotion to produce FM encoding and, perhaps, it is this interaction which generates conditions fundamental to the creation of FMs.

EMOTION, IMPORTANCE AND PLANS

Why should emotion and importance give rise to FMs? One possible explanation is suggested by a recent theory of emotions. Oatley (1988; 1992) and Oatley and Johnson-Laird (1987) outlined a plan-based theory of emotions in which affect is associated with the construction, operation and outcomes of personal plans (a full account of this theory can be found in Oatley, 1992—only a brief outline is presented here). Consider, first, a simple plan which might take the form of a set of constraints, preconditions or goal(s). The goal has with it a set of actions designed to satisfy the various preconditions of the goal and these actions, in turn, have a set of effects the actions are intended to bring about and, of course, a set of effects they actually cause. Thus, a simple plan takes the form of goal–actions–effects. Simple plans can be more complex than this and may entail various sub-goals that have their own actions and effects. In this case, plans may be represented hierarchically (Miller, Galanter, & Pribram, 1960) in a goal "tree", where the main goal of the plan is accomplished by the (successful) satisfaction of sub-goals.

Some comparatively simple and frequently repeated plans may be represented in memory as stereotypical action sequences or scripts (Schank & Abelson, 1977), and Fig. 6.3 provides an example of this for the plan of making a cup of tea. Plans in human cognition are, however, rarely so simple and instead often feature multiple goals, the specification of some or all of which may be vague rather than specific. Moreover, plans in human cognition are generated on the basis of imperfect knowledge of the world, they are limited by finite resources, and often involve more than one person. Even more importantly, plans are dynamic and depend critically on feedback (see Oatley, 1992, p. 32, table 1). Figure 6.4 illustrates the multiple-goal nature of plans in human cognition for some aspects of a fictitious set of work-related goals.

What happens when plans go wrong or when goals are attained? Both outcomes cause a juncture in goal attainment and, according to the plan-based theory of emotions, these junctures are responded to by emotional reactions. By this view, emotions serve a communicative

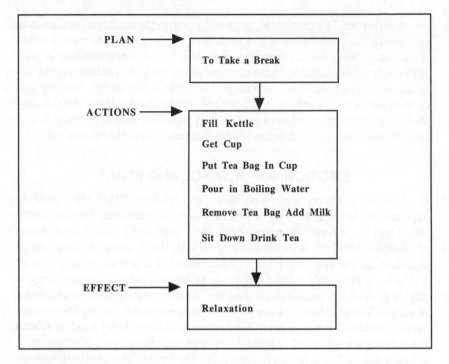

FIG. 6.3. A simple plan.

function and signal that goal structures require repair, reconfiguration or abandonment. Oatley (1992, p. 46) comments that "Emotions insert problems into consciousness, so that the individual can use a model of the system to help integrate new pieces with existing parts of the system". For example, in Fig. 6.3 goal actions may be disrupted and the plan temporarily or permanently abandoned when a goal action is frustrated. Perhaps the individual is out of tea, in which case a moment's irritation may arise or some other emotion associated with frustration may be experienced. Whatever the case, the feeling signals that the plan must be reconfigured. Similarly, but possibly more significantly, a goal may be blocked in Fig. 6.4 when it transpires that a work project cannot be completed on time. More intense, long-lasting and diverse emotions may be experienced here, which signal the repair or change of a whole set of interlinked multiple goals that impinge directly upon central constructs of the self.

Events which lead to FMs virtually always involve plan disruption of one form or another. Sometimes these disruptions affect society, and the public history as a whole (as in the assassination of political leaders), and the emotions caused signal a reconfiguration of an individual's model of

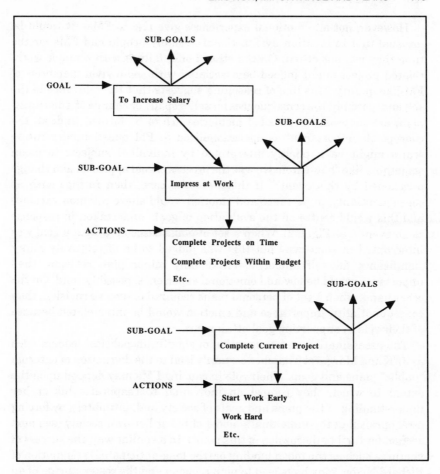

FIG. 6.4. A complex plan.

the public world. Other FM events which are more personal in nature, such as the experience of trauma, may cause emotions which signal and lead to far-reaching changes to the goals of the self. Indeed, it is notable that many victims of repeated and long-lasting trauma (e.g. survivors of childhood trauma, torture, concentration camp prisoners, etc.) often describe attempts to maintain the central goals and plans of the self by creating a private self which is somehow separate from the self-as-victim. The link here between childhood abuse and the clinical syndrome of multiple personality disorder further suggests radical bifurcations of goal structures arising, perhaps, from intense and often repeated emotional experiences that signalled complete restructuring of all major personal goals.

However, not all emotional experiences give rise to FMs—it would be unusual (not to mention dysfunctional) if many people had FMs for the time they ran out of tea. On the other hand, failure with a major work-related project might indeed be associated with some vivid memories of FM-like quality. This line of reasoning suggests that the relevance to the self and, possibly, the consequences for self "repair" or change of a disrupted plan, are necessary if detailed memories are to be formed. Indeed, the concept of "importance" as operationalised in FM questionnaire rating scales might be implicitly interpreted by individual subjects to mean something like "how extensive was the process of goal appraisal and change occasioned by this event?" If this were the case, then ratings such as consequentiality, importance and emotion would share common variance and this would centre on the evaluation of goals undertaken in response to an event (see Fig. 6.2). When a set of plans associated with a goal was interrupted in some way but this was judged to be of relatively minor significance for self and/or to entail only minor plan revision, then importance would be low and emotional experience, possibly, mild. On the other hand, when a set of personal plans required extensive revision, then consequentiality, importance and emotion would be interrelated because of their role in supporting goal attainment.

The assassination and resignation of significant political leaders such as JFK and Margaret Thatcher certainly lead to the disruption of external "public" plans and goals. Their role in causing FMs may depend upon the extent to which they compel an individual to reappraise his or her understanding of the plans and goals of society and, ultimately, by forcing a reappraisal of the individual's model of his or her own society (see next section for further discussion of this point). In a similar way, the success of ventures such as the moon landing or (the long-anticipated) resignation of Richard Nixon, may have lead to plan revision and the restructuring of an individual's model of the goals and plans of society—certainly the Nixon resignation would appear to have given rise to such reappraisals. Ultimately, these disjunctions force a revision of how the plans and goals of the individual fit that individual's model of the goal structure of his or her society. It should be emphasised here that reappraisal of plans and goals does not inevitably lead to negative emotions. For instance, an individual may have been pleased, delighted or gleeful at the resignations of Thatcher or Nixon. The important point is that these emotions were generated because some set of plans changed—perhaps the individual in question no longer had constantly to hope for the downfall of these political leaders. It is only in the case of low-intensity emotional responses, when a revision of personal plans has not occurred, that according to the plan-based view of FMs no detailed durable memories would be formed. Undoubtedly, however, events which directly engage personal plans and goals (events that lead to "real" FMs; see Chapter 4) are far more powerful in eliciting vivid, flashbulb memories and this may be because of the radical revision of self-relevant plans caused by certain types of personal experience.

In Chapter 5, two neuroanatomical routes mediating FM formation were considered and one of these, the amygdala route, was heavily implicated in emotional experience. As detailed in Chapter 5, the amygdala has pathways to the frontal lobes, an area known to be involved in planning. Patients with damage to areas of the frontal lobes often show impairments in generating and executing plans (Shallice, 1988). Also, other areas of the frontal lobes have been thought to be involved in aspects of personality. For example, the neurosurgical excision of parts of the frontal lobes was, at one time, used to subdue emotional aspects of personality (Stuss & Benson, 1984). These observations suggest a potential connection between plans and goals, the self, and emotions. If circuits in the amygdala generate emotion, then possibly this is in response to and/or is modulated by processes in the frontal lobe regions that support goal evaluation. As these putative processes must also have close associations with other frontal regions involved in personality, then it is possible that this route is particularly sensitive to changes to self-relevant plans and goals. Because of the connection to the amygdala, such a neuroanatomical circuit could feature strongly in the encoding of FMs and, perhaps, it is in this way that detailed and durable memories of events associated with goal attainment come to be encoded into long-term memory.

FUNCTIONS OF FLASHBULB MEMORIES

Previous researchers have proposed rather limited functions for FMs. Brown and Kulik (1977) suggested that FMs served the beneficial function of preserving detailed accounts of personally significant events. In contrast, Neisser (1982) argued that FMs represented a critical link between autobiographical memory and the public history—between individual selves and society. It seems likely that FMs fulfil both these functions and a variety of other functions too. As implied above, FMs may take some central role in autobiographical memory generally, they may enter into interpersonal discourse in particular ways, and they may be associated with certain cultural aspects of memory. Each of these three broad domains of FM functions will now be briefly considered.

Flashbulb Memories as Reference Points

Barsalou (1988) and Conway (1992; 1993) proposed that certain types of autobiographical knowledge represent information relating to goal attainment. These authors suggested that information directly concerned with appraisals and evaluations of the goals of the self, is represented at a high level in the autobiographical knowledge base, which does not itself directly encompass knowledge of specific and unique events. However, recent work by Robinson (1992) shows knowledge of specific events and knowledge of goal attainment to be closely interwoven (see Chapter 4). In Robinson's (1992) study of "mini-histories" (Chapter 4), such as "learning to drive a car", it was found that they are comprised of vivid memories of highly specific episodes directly relating to the ease/difficulty of acquisition and to the implications of this for the self. Detailed, vivid, FM-like memories of episodes of skill acquisition carried with them important self-evaluations and when sub-plans were disrupted by failure to acquire skills these evaluations were negative. Emotions associated with mastery of the skill—goal attainment—were positive and many of Robinson's (1992) subjects had FM memories of, for example, the first time they drove a car alone.

Robinson (1992) also noted the vivid nature of memories for first-time experiences and others too have observed a preponderance of FMs to first-time experiences (e.g. Pillemer et al., 1988; in press b; Rubin & Kozin, 1984; see Chapter 4). Flashbulb memories for first-time experiences may retain critical information about plan implementation during periods of transition when new goal structures are being developed. This general association of FMs with plans and goals further suggests that FMs may be important in the overall organisation of autobiographical memory. If, as argued above, FMs arise in response to junctures in plans, then clearly they will represent knowledge which is of both specific and general significance to the rememberer. Such knowledge, apart from providing vital information about plan restructuring, might also serve as an organising component of autobiographical memory by providing cues to other records of the consequences and outcomes of related episodes of plan restructuring (cf. Schank, 1982). According to this view, one function of FMs in autobiographical memory might be to act as *reference points* in the autobiographical memory knowledge base—points at which knowledge of personally relevant goals and associated plans can be directly accessed and then used to explore related knowledge structures.

Communicating with Flashbulb Memories

Pillemer (1992b) provided one of the first thorough discussions of how FMs are used in various types of discourse and argued that a central use is in *persuasion*. According to this view, recounting a FM may add credibility to a person's claim to have actually experienced a particular type of event, experienced an event in a particular way, or to have detailed personal knowledge of a significant event. Neisser's (1982) argument that FMs represent the point at which we line up our personal history with the history of our times and, in effect, say "I was there", would seem to fit with this notion of the persuasive function of FMs. It is worth noting that recounting a FM may not only lead an audience to believe that the rememberer has accurate and detailed knowledge, but it may also convince the rememberer herself that the event was actually experienced and that it was experienced in the way it is recalled. Bell and Loftus (1989) found that the recall of minor but highly specific details can have an inordinate impact on jurors' belief in the accuracy of an eyewitness account. So marked was this effect that Bell and Loftus (1989) referred to it as *trivial persuasion,* to capture the notion that the recounting of apparently trivial details leads the audience to infer that a rememberer is accurate in his or her recall.

Apart from persuasion, accounts of FMs in discourse may serve other functions too. Pillemer (1992b) proposes that FM accounts may raise the intimacy and emotionality of a discourse and draw the recipients into a closer interpersonal interaction. Pillemer (1992b) sites Beals' (1991) study in which it was found that students interacting with academic members of staff over a computer network were more likely to evoke a response from their tutors and fellow students when a specific and detailed learning-related episode was recounted than when more general course-related problems were raised. The intimacy function of detailed and vivid autobiographical memories in discourse may, however, be just one aspect of the strategic use of FMs in interpersonal communication. Everyday experience and observation suggests that recounting detailed memories is often linked to strategic self-disclosures that may be used to facilitate or even inhibit further social interaction.

In an intriguing study, Hyman and Faries (1992) investigated the types of memories people frequently talked about and the situations in which they did so. In this study, subjects described both their memories and details of events in which they had recounted the memories. Figure 6.5 shows the distribution of memories categorised into memory types by Hyman and Faries (1992, pp. 210–211). The four most frequent types of memories were "my experience with X", "self-description", "point illustration" and "current events". Memories in the "my experience with X" group were dominated by accounts which arose when the rememberer, in the course of an interaction, reached a point where he or she could relate his or her own story on the current discourse topic. For instance, one subject noted that he talked about his first date (with his current partner) when the topic of first dates came up in conversation with friends. Another subject described a student prank he had taken part in during a conversation with friends concerning strange things they had done when

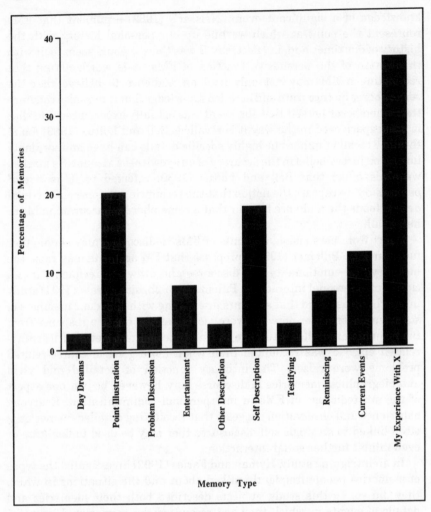

FIG. 6.5. Uses of autobiographical memories in interpersonal interactions (after Hyman & Faries, 1992, fig. 1).

they had been students. Another frequent type of "my experience with X" memories were earliest memories and these were recalled in conversations about earliest recollections. Presumably, many of these memories would have been highly vivid and detailed memories with a FM-quality and it seems their function was to promote close interpersonal relations by identifying common experiences and sharing these.

In the "point illustration" class, memories provided examples of past experiences and were used to give advice. Hyman and Faries (1992) comment that one of their subjects described how he had survived an attack by killer bees and how he often recounted this memory to colleagues who worked with him in the study of bees. The third frequent class of "self-description" memories referred to self-disclosures (often of FMs) that were aimed at explaining or describing self to (significant) others. Finally, the class "current events" primarily included the use of specific recollections to inform others of current changes and goals in a person's life. The study by Hyman and Faries (1992) was not specifically focused on FMs, although some of the memories they sampled certainly were FMs; nevertheless, their findings suggest that one major function of recounting memories is to promote and develop interpersonal relations. A second function would appear to be to inform others about plans and goals relating to possible contingencies in everyday experience or, more idiosyncratically, to self. Flashbulb memories, given that they retain detailed and significant goal attainment information, may be particularly potent in promoting these functions of social intimacy and plan sharing.

Cultural Effects of Flashbulb Memories

Significant cultural events can give rise to the widespread formation of FMs within a society (Chapters 1 and 3) and these have been referred to as "collective" memories (see, e.g. Connerton, 1989; Middleton & Edwards, 1990). Events that promote collective memories are often associated with widespread discussion within a society generally at the time of occurrence of a culturally significant event. Later an event may be commemorated by monuments, and in books and films. However, the public marking of a significant cultural event does not necessarily take place immediately or even soon after the event. For example, in the case of traumatic public events, the actual location of the event may not become marked by monuments or other types of reminders. Pennebaker (submitted) observed that in Dallas in the years following the assassination of JFK, virtually no monuments were erected nor were streets named after the murdered President, although this type of commemoration was common in other cities in North America. A similar type of public "denial" also occurred in Memphis, Tennessee, the location of the murder of Martin Luther King. However, approximately 25 years after the two assassinations, both cities finally acknowledged the leaders murdered in their cities with fairly extravagant memorial centres. Possibly, this lag in commemoration reflects a period of restructuring in which the traumatic event is gradually reconceptualised—as in memory for personal trauma.

Pennebaker (submitted) and his colleagues investigated this further in a survey of a wide range of positive and negative public events for the date of the erection of monuments compared with the date of actual occurrence of the events commemorated. It was found that the lag between event and monument followed a regular 20–30 year cycle and this was the case for both positive and negative cultural events. The lag between movies of events and date of occurrence was also examined and again it was found that most (historical) movies refer to events that took place approximately 20 years prior to the making of the movie.

Pennebaker considers a number of interrelated explanations for this 20- to 25-year cycle in commemorating cultural events. One account concerns the notion that there is a critical period in the formation of identity (self, social and political identity) which occurs between the ages of about 15–25 years (Erikson, 1950; 1978; see Schuman & Rieger, 1992, for memory data supporting this notion and Conway & Rubin, 1993, for a review). The suggestion is that people in this age group are undergoing the process of identity formation and, as a consequence, are more likely to be strongly affected by major cultural events than younger or older subjects. One way in which this might be evident would be in a higher frequency of FMs among people who were between the ages of 15–25 years when a significant cultural event occurred (see Chapters 3 and 4 for some evidence supporting this suggestion). However, 15- to 25-year-olds are not immediately in a position to commemorate the public events significant to their age group and must wait 20 years or more until their generation fills the positions of power within society and can then initiate the public commemoration of the events of cultural significance for their generation. One function of FMs, then, might be in supporting this cyclic collective "remembering" of public events that were critical in the formation of the identity of a generation. Vivid, durable FMs for cultural events that featured significantly in the emergence of identity will be retained by the rememberer until he or she is in a position to publicly commemorate the critical events and in this way FMs may support generational identity and the expression of that identity.

CONCLUSIONS:
THE MULTIFUNCTIONALITY OF
FLASHBULB MEMORIES

Brown and Kulik (1977) outlined a clear and essentially simple model that identified the nature, genesis and function of a special type of memory that they named "flashbulb" memory. On the basis of the evidence reviewed in earlier chapters, it is clear that Brown and Kulik were correct: there is a distinct class of memories for events that are emotional and personally important and, sometimes, surprising. These memories are more detailed and long-lasting than most everyday autobiographical memories, they play a central role in autobiographical memory generally, support many different uses of memory in interpersonal interaction, and may facilitate cultural processes such as the expression of generational identity. Furthermore, the evidence from neurobiological studies of memory, although provisional at this stage nevertheless strongly points to the possibility of some type of preferential encoding of FMs. Given this broad pattern of findings, it seems reasonable to conclude that the FMH requires revision rather than rejection. The main revision I have suggested is that the relation between FMs and goals and plans should form a more central component of the FMH: flashbulb memories are records of moments when personally important plans required urgent revision. They are accurate because knowledge of plan review and change must be accurate if it is to be of any worth and they are durable because knowledge of previous plan revision supports efficient plan change in the future. Finally, so critical is the preservation records of goal attainment that specialised brain systems may have been developed for the encoding of such information.

References

American Psychiatric Association. (1986). *Diagnostic and Statistical Manual of Mental Disorders (DSM-IIIR),* 3rd edn. Washington, DC: APA.

Anderson, J.R. (1987). Skill acquisition: Compilation of weak-method problem solutions. *Psychological Review, 94,* 192–210.

Anderson, S.J. (1993). *Investigating the structure of autobiographical memory.* Doctoral dissertation, Department of Psychology, University of Lancaster.

Anderson, S.J., & Conway, M.A. (1993). Investigating the structure of autobiographical memories. *Journal of Experimental Psychology: Learning, Memory, and Cognition, 19,* 1178–1196.

Baddeley, A.D. (1986). *Working memory.* Oxford: Clarendon Press.

Baddeley, A.D., & Wilson, B. (1986). Amnesia, autobiographical memory, and confabulation. In D.C. Rubin (Ed.), *Autobiographical memory,* pp. 225–252. Cambridge: Cambridge University Press.

Barsalou, L.W. (1988). The content and organization of autobiographical memories. In U. Neisser & E. Winograd (Eds.), *Remembering reconsidered: Ecological and traditional approaches to the study of memory.* (pp. 193–243). New York: Cambridge University Press.

Beals, D.E. (1991). Stories form the classroom: Rate of response to personal event narratives told by beginning teachers. *Quarterly Newsletter of the Laboratory of Comparative Human Cognition, 13,* 31–38.

Bell, B.E., & Loftus, E.F. (1989). Trivial persuasion in the courtroom: The power of (a few) minor details. *Journal of Personality and Social Psychology, 56,* 669–679.

Bentler, P.M. (1980). Multivariate analysis with latent variables: Causal modelling. *Annual Review of Psychology, 31,* 419–456.

Bentler, P.M. (1989). *EQS: Structural Equations Program Manual*. Los Angeles, CA: BMDP Statistical Software.

Bentler, P.M., & Weeks, D.G. (1980). Linear structural equations with latent variables. *Psychometrika, 45*, 289–308.

Bliss, T.V.P., & Lomo, T. (1973). Long-lasting potentiation of synaptic transmission in the dentate area of the anaesthetized rabbit following stimulation of the perforant path. *Journal of Physiology, 232*, 331–356.

Bohannon, J.N. (1988). Flashbulb memories for the Space Shuttle disaster: A tale of two theories. *Cognition, 29*, 179–196.

Brewer, W.F. (1988). Memory for randomly sampled autobiographical events. In U. Neisser & E. Winograd (Eds.), *Remembering reconsidered: Ecological and traditional approaches to the study of memory*, pp. 21–90. New York: Cambridge University Press.

Brewin, C.R., Andrews, B., & Gotlib, I.H. (1993). Psychopathology and early experience: A reappraisal of retrospective reports. *Psychological Bulletin, 133*, 82–98.

Brown, N. (1990). Organization of public events in long-term memory. *Journal of Experimental Psychology: General, 119*, 297–314.

Brown, R., & Kulik, J. (1977). Flashbulb memories. *Cognition, 5*, 73–99.

Brown, T.H., Chapman, P.F., Kairiss, E.W., & Keenan, C.L. (1988). Long-term synaptic potentiation. *Science, 242*, 724–728.

Bunuel, L. (1985). *My last breath*. London: Fontana.

Christianson, S.-A. (1989). Flashbulb memories: Special, but not so special. *Memory and Cognition, 17*, 435–443.

Christianson, S.-A. (1992). Emotional stress and eyewitness memory: A critical review. *Psychological Bulletin, 112*, 284–309.

Christianson, S.-A., & Nilsson, L.-G. (1989). Hysterical amnesia: A case of aversively motivated isolation of memory. In T. Archer & L.-G. Nilsson (Eds.), *Aversion, avoidance, and anxiety: Perspectives on aversively motivated behaviour*, pp. 289–310. Hillsdale, NJ: Lawrence Elrbaum Associates Inc.

Cohen, G., & Faulkner, D. (1987). Life span changes in autobiographical memory. *Human Cognition Research Laboratory, Technical Report No. 24*.

Cohen, G., Conway, M.A., & Maylor, E.A. (in press). Flashbulb memories in older adults. *Psychology and Aging*.

Cohen, N.J., McCloskey, M., & Wible, C.G. (1988). There is still no case for a flashbulb-memory mechanism: Reply to Schmidt and Bohannon. *Journal of Experimental Psychology: General, 117*, 336–338.

Cohen, N.J., McCloskey, M., & Wible, C.G. (1990). Flashbulb memories and underlying cognitive mechanisms: Reply to Pillemer. *Journal of Experimental Psychology: General, 119*, 97–100.

Colegrove, F.W. (1899). Individual memories. *American Journal of Psychology, 10*, 228–255.

Connerton, P. (1989). *How societies remember*. Cambridge: Cambridge University Press.

Conway, M.A. (1988). *Vivid memories of novel, important, and mundane events*. Unpublished manuscript. Applied Psychology Unit, Cambridge.

Conway, M.A. (1990). *Autobiographical memory: An introduction*. Buckingham: Open University Press.

Conway, M.A. (1992). A structural model of autobiographical memory. In M.A. Conway, D.C. Rubin, H. Spinnler, & W.A. Wagenaar (Eds.), *Theoretical perspectives on autobiographical memory*, pp. 167–194. Dordrecht: Kluwer Academic.

Conway, M.A. (1993). Impairments of autobiographical memory. In H. Spinnler & F. Boller (Eds.), *Handbook of neuropsychology*, 8th edn, pp. 175–191. Amsterdam: Elsevier.

Conway, M.A. (in press). Autobiographical knowledge and autobiographical memories. In D.C.Rubin (Ed.), *The construction of autobiographical memory*. Cambridge: Cambridge University Press.

Conway, M.A., & Anderson, S.J. (1993). Are autobiographical memories stable? Manuscript under review.

Conway, M.A., Anderson, S.J., Larsen, S.F., Donnelly, C.M., McDaniel, M.A., McClelland, A.G.R., Rawles, R.E., & Logie, R.H. (1994). The formation of flashbulb memories. *Memory and Cognition, 22*(3), 326–343.

Conway, M.A., & Bekerian, D.A. (1987). Organization in autobiographical memory. *Memory & Cognition, 15*(2), 119–132.

Conway, M.A., & Bekerian, D.A. (1988). Characteristics of vivid memories. In M.M. Gruneberg, P. Morris, R.N. Sykes (Eds.), *Practical aspects of memory: Current research and issues, Vol. 1.* (pp. 519–524). Chichester: Wiley.

Conway, M.A., & Rubin, D.C. (1993). The structure of autobiographical memory. In A.E. Collins, S.E. Gathercole, M.A. Conway, & P.E. Morris (Eds.), *Theories of memory*, pp. 103–137. Hove: Lawrence Erlbaum Associates Ltd.

Conway, M.A., Rubin, D.C., Spinnler, H., & Wagenaar, W.A. (Eds.) (1992). *Theoretical perspectives on autobiographical memory*. Dordrecht: Kluwer Academic.

Dewhurst, S.A., & Conway, M.A. (in press). Pictures, images, and recollective experience. *Journal of Experimental Psychology: Learning, Memory and Cognition*.

Erikson, E. (1950). *Childhood and society*. New York: W.W. Norton.

Erikson, E. (1978). *Adulthood*. New York: W.W. Norton.

Fisher, R.P., Geiselman, R.E., & Amandor, M. (1989). Field test of the cognitive interview: Enhancing the recollection of actual victims and witnesses of crime. *Journal of Applied Psychology, 74,* 722–727.

Fitzgerald, J.M. (1988). Vivid memories and the reminiscence phenomenon: The role of a self narrative. *Human Development, 31,* 261–273.

Fitzgerald, J.M., & Lawrence, R. (1984). Autobiographical memory across the life-span. *Journal of Gerontology, 39,* 692–698.

Foy, D.W. (1992). *Treating PTSD*. New York: Guilford Press.

Geiselman, R.E., Fisher, R.P., MacKinnon, D.P., & Holland, H.L. (1985). Eyewitness memory enhancement in the police interview: Cognitive retrieval mnemonics versus hypnosis. *Journal of Applied Psychology, 70,* 401–412.

Gold, P.E. (1992). A proposed neurobiological basis for regulating memory storage for significant events. In E.Winograd & U.Neisser (Eds.), *Affect and accuracy in recall: Studies of "flashbulb" memories*, pp. 141–161. New York: Cambridge University Press.

Grice, H.P. (1975). Logic and conversation. In P. Cole & J.L. Morgan (Eds.), *Syntax and semantics*, pp. 41–58. New York: Seminar Press.

Heuer, F., & Reisberg, D. (1990). Vivid memories of emotional events: The accuracy of remembered minutiae. *Memory and Cognition, 18,* 496–506.

Horowitz, M.J., & Reidbord, S.P. (1992). Memory, emotion, and response to trauma. In S.-A. Christianson (Ed.), *The handbook of emotion and memory: Research and theory*, pp. 343–358. Hillsdale, NJ: Lawrence Erlbaum Associates Inc.

Horowitz, M.J., Wilner, N., Kaltreider, N., & Alvarez, W. (1980). Signs and symptoms of post-traumatic stress disorder. *Archives of General Psychiatry, 37*, 85–92.

Hyman, I.E., & Faries, J.M. (1992). The functions of autobiographical memory. In M.A. Conway, D.C. Rubin, H. Spinnler, & W.A. Wagenaar (Eds.), *Theoretical perspectives on autobiographical memory*, pp. 207–221. Dordrecht: Kluwer Academic.

Johnson, M.K. (1985). The origin of memories. In P.C. Kendall (Ed.), *Advances in cognitive-behavioural research and therapy*, Vol. 4, pp. 1–27. New York: Academic Press.

Johnson, M.K., Hashtroudi, S., & Lindsay, D.S. (1993). Source monitoring. *Psychological Bulletin, 114*, 3–28.

Kagan, J. (1972). A psychologist's account at mid-career. In T.S. Krawiec (Ed.), *The psychologists*, Vol. 1. New York: Oxford University Press.

Kesner, R.P. (1991). The emergence of multidimensional approaches to the structural organization of memory. In R.G. Lister & H.J. Weingartner (Eds.), *Perspectives on cognitive neuroscience*, pp. 218–228. New York: Oxford University Press.

Kolb, B., & Wishaw, I.Q. (1990). *Fundamentals of human neuropsychology*, 3rd edn. New York: W.H. Freeman.

Kulver, H., & Bucy, P.C. (1937). "Psychic blindness" and other symptoms following bilateral temporal lobectomy in rhesus monkeys. *American Journal of Physiology, 119*, 352–353.

Larsen, S.F. (1992). Potential flashbulbs: Memories of ordinary news as the baseline. In E. Winograd & U. Neisser (Eds.), *Affect and accuracy in recall: Studies of "flashbulb memories"*, pp., 32–64. New York: Cambridge University Press.

LeDoux, J.E. (1992). Emotion and memory: Anatomical systems underlying indelible neural traces. In S.-A. Christianson (Ed.), *The handbook of emotion and memory: Research and theory*, pp. 269–288. Hillsdale, NJ: Lawrence Erlbaum Associates Inc.

Linton, M. (1975). Memory for real-world events. In D.A. Norman & D.E. Rumelhart (Eds.), *Explorations in cognition*, pp. 376–404. San Francisco, CA: W.H. Freeman.

Linton, M. (1982). Transformations of memory in everyday life. In U. Neisser (Ed.), *Memory observed: Remembering in natural contexts*, pp. 77–81. San Francisco, CA: W.H. Freeman.

Livingston, R.B. (1967a). Brain circuitry relating to complex behaviour. In G.C. Quarton, T. Melnechuck, & F.O. Schmitt (Eds.), *The neurosciences: A study program*, pp. 499–514. New York: Rockefeller University Press.

Livingston, R.B. (1967b). Reinforcement. In G.C. Quarton, T. Melnechuck, & F.O. Schmitt (Eds.), *The neurosciences: A study program*, pp. 568–576. New York: Rockefeller University Press.

Loftus, E.F. (1993). The reality of repressed memories. *American Psychologist, 48*, 518–537.

Loftus, E.F., & Kaufman, L. (1992). Why do traumatic experiences sometimes produce good memory (flashbulbs) and sometimes no memory (repression)? In E. Winograd & U. Neisser (Eds.), *Affect and accuracy in recall: Studies of "flashbulb memories"*, pp. 212–223. New York: Cambridge University Press.

Mayes, A.R. (1988). *Human organic memory disorders*. Cambridge: Cambridge University Press.

McCloskey, M., Wible, C.G., & Cohen, N.J. (1988). Is there a special flashbulb-memory mechanism? *Journal of Experimental Psychology: General, 117*, 171–181.

McGaugh, J.L. (1991). Neuromodulation and the storage of information: Involvement of the amygdaloid complex. In R.G. Lister & H.J. Weingartner (Eds.), *Perspectives on cognitive neuroscience*, pp. 279–299. New York: Oxford University Press.

McGaugh, J.L. (1992). Affect, neuromodulatory systems, and memory storage. In S.-A. Christianson (Ed.), *The handbook of emotion and memory: Research and theory*, pp. 245–268. Hillsdale, NJ: Lawrence Erlbaum Associates Inc.

McGaugh, J.L., Introini-Collison, I.B., Naghara, A.H., & Cahill, L. (1989). Involvement of the amygdala in hormonal and neurotransmitter interactions in the modulation of memory storage. In T. Archer & L.-G. Nilsson (Eds.), *Aversion, avoidance, and anxiety: Perspectives on aversively motivated behaviour*, pp. 231–250. Hillsdale, NJ: Lawrence Erlbaum Associates Inc.

Middleton, D., & Edwards, D. (1990). *Collective remembering*. London: Sage.

Miller, G.A., Galanter, E., & Pribram, K.H. (1960). *Plans and the structure of behavior*. New York: Holt, Reinhart and Winston.

Mishkin, M. (1982). A memory system in the monkey. *Philosophical Transactions of the Royal Society, B298*, 85–95.

Mishkin, M., & Appenzeller, T. (1987). The anatomy of memory. *Scientific American, 256*, 62–71.

Moos, R.H. (1977). *Menstrual Distress Questionnaire manual*. Stanford, CA: Social Ecology Laboratory, Stanford University.

Neisser, U. (1982). Snapshots or benchmarks? In U. Neisser (Ed.), *Memory observed: Remembering in natural contexts*, pp. 43–48. San Francisco, CA: W.H. Freeman.

Neisser, U. (1986). Remembering Pearl Habor: Reply to Thompson and Cowan. *Cognition, 23*, 285–286.

Neisser, U. (1988). Commentary. *Human Development, 31*, 271–273.

Neisser, U., & Harsch, N. (1992). Phantom flashbulbs: False recollections of hearing the news about *Challenger*. In E.Winograd & U. Neisser (Eds.), *Affect and accuracy in recall: Studies of "flashbulb memories"*, pp. 9–31. Cambridge: Cambridge University Press.

Neisser, U., Winograd, E., & Weldon, M.S. (1991). Remembering the earthquake: "What I experienced" vs. "How I heard the news". Paper presented to the *Psychonomic Society*, San Francisco, CA, November.

Norman, D.A., & Bobrow, D.G. (1979). Descriptions: An intermediate stage in memory retrieval. *Cognitive Psychology, 11*, 107–123.

Norman, D.A., & Shallice, T. (1980). Attention to action: Willed and automatic control of behaviour. *Technical Report No. 99*, University of California, San Diego.

Oatley, K. (1988). Plans and the communicative function of emotions: A cognitive theory. In V. Hamilton, G.H. Bower, & N.H. Frijda (Eds.), *Cognitive perspectives on emotion and motivation*. Dordrecht: Kluwer Academic.

Oatley, K. (1992). *The best laid schemes: The psychology of emotions*. Cambridge: Cambridge University Press.

Oatley, K., & Johnson-Laird, P.N. (1987). Towards a cognitive theory of emotions. *Cognition and Emotion, 1*, 29–50.

Parkin, A.J. (1987). *Memory and amnesia: An introduction*. Oxford: Basil Blackwell.

Parkin, A.J., & Leng, R.C. (1993). *Neuropsychology of the amnesic syndrome*. Hove: Lawrence Erlbaum Associates Ltd.

Pennebaker, J.W. (submitted). On the creation and maintenance of collective memories.

Pillemer, D.B. (1984). Flashbulb memories of the assassination attempt on President Reagan. *Cognition, 16*, 63–80.

Pillemer, D.B. (1990). Clarifying the flashbulb memory concept: A comment on McCloskey, Wible, and Cohen (1988). *Journal of Experimental Psychology: General, 119*, 92–96.

Pillemer, D.B. (1992a). Preschool children's memories of personal circumstances: The fire alarm study. In E. Winograd & U. Neisser (Eds.), *Affect and accuracy in recall: Studies of "flashbulb memories"*, pp. 121–140. Cambridge: Cambridge University Press.

Pillemer, D.B. (1992b). Remembering personal circumstances: A functional analysis. In E.Winograd & U. Neisser (Eds.), *Affect and accuracy in recall: Studies of "flashbulb memories"*, pp. 236–264. Cambridge: Cambridge University Press.

Pillemer, D.B., Goldsmith, L.R., Panter, A.T., & White, S.H. (1988). Very long-term memories of the first year in college. *Journal of Experimental Psychology: Learning, Memory and Cognition, 14*, 709–715.

Pillemer, D.B., Rinehart, E.D., & White, S.H. (1986). Memories of life transitions: The first year in college. *Human Learning, 5*, 109–123.

Pillemer, D.B., Koff, E., Rinehart, E.D., & Rierdan, J. (1987). Flashbulb memories of menarche and adult menstrual distress. *Journal of Adolescence, 10*, 187–199.

Pillemer, D.B., Picariello, M.L., & Pruett, J.C. (in press a). Very long-term memories of a salient preschool event. *Applied Cognitive Psychology*.

Pillemer, D.B., Picariello, M.L., Law, A.B., & Reichman, J.S. (in press b). Memories of college: The importance of specific educational episodes. In D.C. Rubin (Ed.), *The construction of autobiographical memories*. Cambridge: Cambridge University Press.

Robinson, J.A. (1992). First experience memories: Contexts and functions in personal histories. In M.A. Conway, D.C. Rubin, H. Spinnler, & W.A. Wagenaar (Eds.), *Theoretical perspectives on autobiographical memory*, pp. 223–239. Dordrecht: Kluwer Academic.

Ross, M. (1989). Relation of implicit theories to the construction of personal histories. *Psychological Review, 96*, 341–357.

Rubin, D.C. (Ed.) (1986). *Autobiographical memory*. Cambridge: Cambridge University Press.

Rubin, D.C. (Ed.) (in press). *The construction of autobiographical memories*. Cambridge: Cambridge University Press.

Rubin, D.C., & Kozin, M. (1984). Vivid memories. *Cognition, 16*, 81–95.

Schank, R.C. (1982). *Dynamic memory*. New York: Cambridge University Press.

Schank, R.C., & Abelson, R.P. (1977). *Scripts, plans, goals, and understanding*. Hillsdale, NJ: Lawrence Erlbaum Associates Inc.

Schmidt, S.R., & Bohannon, J.N. (1988). In defense of the flashbulb-memory hypothesis: A comment on McCloskey, Wible, and Cohen. *Journal of Experimental Psychology: General, 117*, 332–335.

Schuman, H., & Rieger, C. (1992). Collective memory and collective memories. In M.A. Conway, D.C. Rubin, H. Spinnler, & W. Wagenaar (Eds.), *Theoretical perspectives on autobiographical memory*, pp. 323–336. Dordrecht: Kluwer Academic.

Scoville, A.F., & Milner, B. (1957). Loss of recent memory after bilateral hippocampal lesions. *Journal of Neurology, Neurosurgery and Psychiatry, 20*, 11–12.

Shallice, T. (1988). *From neuropsychology to mental structure*. New York: Cambridge University Press.

Sheingold, K., & Tenny, Y.T. (1982). Memory for a salient childhood event. In U. Neisser (Ed.), *Memory observed: Remembering in natural contexts*, pp. 201–212. San Francisco, CA: W.H. Freeman.

Squire, L.R. (1992). Memory and the hippocampus: A synthesis from findings with rats, monkeys, and humans. *Psychological Review, 99*, 195–231.

Stuss, D.T., & Benson, D.F. (1984). Neuropsychological studies of the frontal lobes. *Psychological Bulletin, 95*, 3–28.

Terr, L.C. (1979). Children of Chowchilla: A study of psychic trauma. *Psychoanalysis. Study Child, 34*, 547–623.

Terr, L.C. (1983). Chowchilla revisited: The effects of psychic trauma four years after a school bus kidnapping. *American Journal of Psychiatry, 140*, 1543–1550.

Terr, L.C. (1988). What happens to early memories of trauma? A study of 20 children under age five at the time of documented traumatic events. *Journal of the American Academy of Child and Adolescent Psychiatry, 27*, 96–104.

Terr, L.C. (1991). Childhood traumas: An outline and overview. *American Journal of Psychiatry, 148*, 10–19.

Thompson, C.P., & Cowan, T. (1986). Flashbulb memories: A nicer interpretation of a Neisser recollection. *Cognition, 22*, 199–200.

Usher, J.A., & Neisser, U. (1993). Childhood amnesia and the beginnings of memory for four early life events. *Journal of Experimental Psychology: General, 122*, 155–165.

Wagenaar, W.A., & Groeneweg, J. (1990). The memory of concentration camp survivors. *Applied Cognitive Psychology, 4*, 77–87.

Walker, M. (1992). *Surving secrets*. Buckingham: Open University Press.

Weaver, C.A. (1993). Do you need a "flash" to form a flashbulb memory? *Journal of Experimental Psychology: General, 122*, 39–46.

White, R.T. (1982). Memory for personal events. *Human Learning, 1*, 171–183.

Williams, D.M., & Hollan, J.D. (1981). The process of retrieval from very long-term memory. *Cognitive Science, 5*, 87–119.

Winograd, E., & Killinger, W.A., Jr. (1983). Relating age at encoding in early childhood to adult recall: Development of flashbulb memories. *Journal of Experimental Psychology: General, 112*, 413–422.

Wright, D.B. (1993). Recall of the Hillsborough disaster over time: Systematic biases of "flashbulb" memories. *Applied Cognitive Psychology, 7,* 129–138.

Yarmey, A.D., & Bull, M.P. (1978). Where were you when President Kennedy was assassinated? *Bulletin of the Psychonomic Society, 11,* 133–135.

Yerkes, R.M., & Dodson, J.D. (1908). The relation of strength of stimulus to rapidity of habit-formation. *Journal of Comparative Neurology of Psychology, 18,* 459–482.

Yuille, J.C., & Cutshall, J.L. (1986). A case study of eyewitness memory of a crime. *Journal of Applied Psychology, 71,* 291–301.

Author Index

Abelson, R.P., 117
Alvarez, W., 81
American Psychiatric Association., 80
Anderson, J.R., 111
Anderson, S.J., 26, 53–66, 110–111
Andrews, B., 81
Appenzeller, T., 97–98
Baddeley, A.D., 21, 102–103
Beals, D.E., 123
Bekerian, D.A., 70
Bell, B.E., 123
Benson, D.F., 21, 102–103
Bentler, P.M., 61
Bliss, T.V.P., 103
Bobrow, D.G., 58
Bohannon, J.N., 27, 30–33
Brewer, B.F., 19
Brewin, C.R., 81, 110
Brown, N., 5, 61
Brown, R., 1–15, 18–25, 44, 63–65,
    81–82, 109, 112, 121–126
Brown, T.H., 104
Bucy, P.C. 101
Bull, M.P., 1, 82
Bunuel, L., 18
Cahill, L., 100
Chapman, P.F., 104
Christianson, S.-A., 25–25, 38, 67,

78–79, 81
Cohen, G., 87–91
Cohen, N.J., 33
Colegrove, F.W., 25
Connerton, P., 125
Conway, M.A., 26, 53–67, 70, 73, 76,
    87–91, 97, 103, 106, 110–111, 121
Cowan, T., 21
Cutshall, J.L., 76–78, 112
Dewhurst, S.A., 106
Dodson, J.D., 25
Donnelly, C.M., 53–66
Edwards, D., 125
Erikson, E., 126
Faries, J.M., 123–125
Faulkner, D., 91
Fisher, R.P., 35
Fitzgerald, J.M., 91
Foy, D.W., 81
Galanter, E., 117
Geiselman, R.E., 35
Gold, P.E., 104
Goldsmith, L.R., 71
Gotlib, I.H., 81
Grice, H.P., 26
Groeneweg, J., 90–91, 112
Harsch, N., 19, 32–34, 49, 52, 58
Hastroudi, S., 106

Heuer, F., 24
Hollan, J.D., 58
Holland, H.L., 35
Horowitz, M.J., 81
Hyman, I.E., 123–125
Introini-Collinson, I.B., 100
Johnson-Laird, P.N., 117
Johnson, M.K., 19, 22, 106
Kagan, J., 73
Kairiss, E.W., 104
Kaltreider, N., 81
Kaufman, L., 81
Keenan, C.L., 104
Kesner, R.P., 106–107
Killinger, W.A., 82–83
Kluver, H., 101
Koff, E., 75
Kolb, B., 95, 97
Kozin, M., 32, 54, 91, 121
Kulik, J., 1–15, 18–25, 44, 63–65,
   81–82, 109, 112, 121–126
Larsen, S.F., 3, 5, 53–66
Law, A.B., 97
Lawrence, R., 91
LeDoux, J.E., 95, 101
Leng, R.C., 97, 102
Lindsay, D.S., 106
Linton, M., 19, 112
Livingston, R.B., 13, 81, 95–96, 106
Loftus, E.F., 21, 123
Logie, R.H., 53–66
Lomo, T., 103
MacKinnon, D.P., 35
Mayes, A.R., 97
Maylor, E.A., 87–90
McClelland, A.G.R., 53–66
McCloskey, M., 33, 67, 110
McDaniel, M.A., 53–66
McGaugh, J.L., 100–101
Middleton, D., 125
Miller, G.A., 97, 117
Milner, B., 97
Mishkin, M., 97–98
Moos, R.H., 75
Naghara, A.H., 100
Neisser, U., 17–27, 32–38, 49–52, 58,
   66–67, 86, 121
Nilsson, L.-G., 78–79
Norman, D.A., 58, 103

Oatley, K., 117–119
Panter, A.T., 71
Parkin, A.J., 97, 102
Pennebaker, J.W., 125
Picariello, M.L., 84
Pillemer, D.B., 33, 39, 43–49, 53,
   66–67, 71, 75, 84–86, 121, 122–123
Pribram, K.H., 117
Pruett, J.C., 84
Rawles, R.E., 53–66
Reichman, J.S., 84
Reidbord, S.P., 81
Reisberg, D., 24
Rieger, C., 53
Rierdan, J., 75
Rinehart, E.D., 71, 75
Robinson, J.A., 76, 80, 121
Ross, M., 21
Rubin, D.C., 32, 54, 76, 91, 110, 121
Schank, R.C., 48, 61, 117
Schmidt, S.R., 33
Schuman, H., 53
Scoville, A.F., 97
Shallice, T., 21, 102–103, 121
Sheingold, K., 86
Spinnler, H., 99
Squire, L.R., 97–100
Stuss, D.T., 21, 102, 121
Tenny, Y.T., 86
Terr, L.C., 79–81, 86–87, 110, 112–114
Thompson, C.P., 21
Usher, J.A., 86
Wagenaar, W.A., 90–91, 112
Walker, M., 80, 112
Weaver, C.A., 39
Weeks, D.G., 61
Weldon, M.S., 49
White, R.T., 19
White, S.H., 71
Wible, C.G., 33
Williams, D.M., 58
Wilner, N., 81
Wilson, B., 21, 102
Winograd, E., 49, 82–83
Wishaw, I.Q., 95, 97
Wright, D.B., 40–41, 75
Yarmey, A.D., 1, 82
Yerkes, R.M., 25
Yuille, J.C., 76–78, 112

Subject Index

accuracy, 14–15, 17–22, 33–34, 40, 77–78, 90–91, 109–110

amnesia, 10, 25, 76–79, 97–98

amygdala, 97–103

arousal, 17, 24–25

attribute/consistency scores, 35, 47–59, 87–88

autobiographical memories, 3, 25–27, 30, 76, 91, 110–111

biological significance, 13–14, 95

brain circuits, 15, 97–107

canonical categories, 5–6, 9, 13–14, 17, 25–29, 32, 34, 44, 49, 51–52, 68, 71, 82, 84

Challenger, 27–39, 50–58

confabulated, 20–21, 102–103

consequentiality, 4–5, 7–9, 11–15, 17, 19–24, 27, 30–34, 37–40, 48, 52, 63–69, 72, 74, 76, 92, 114–117

correlation(al), 9, 12, 23, 38, 40, 47, 70, 75

details/ed/s, 3–4, 6, 14–17, 21–29, 45, 49, 59, 67–68, 77, 79, 86, 90–91

durability/durable, 1, 14, 23, 26, 29, 45, 48, 67, 77, 90–107, 112

elaboration, 10–11, 13, 15

emotion(al), 29–31, 38–40, 47–48, 52, 68–72, 90, 114–117

emotion/affect intensity of, 31, 38–39, 44, 52, 60–65, 74–76, 79, 92

encoding, 10, 13–14, 17–19, 22–23, 30–33, 40, 66, 83, 95

errors, 35–38, 58–59, 79, 81

event features, 4–6, 14–15, 29, 34, 39, 81

everyday/ordinary memories, 19, 33, 39, 110–111

flashbulb memories
  account(s)/descriptions, 1, 5, 6, 13, 18–19, 22, 25–26, 35, 57, 59, 71–73, 82, 87
  content/organisation, 17, 22, 25, 110–114
  FMs, 1, 3–7, 9–11, 23–29, 32–33, 38, 40–41, 43–54, 60–68, 70–72, 75, 77–82, 86–87, 120
  formation of, 9–18, 20–23, 27, 38–39, 49, 60–66, 77, 90–92, 95–107, 114–117
  frequency of, 4, 6, 9, 14, 30, 41, 47, 50–54, 81, 90–92
  uses/functions, 14, 17–18, 26, 73, 109, 121–126

Flashbulb Memory Hypothesis (FMH), 3, 10–14, 17–19, 22–27, 33–34, 38–43, 48–49, 52–53, 56, 60–66, 68, 90–92

forgotten, 33, 37–38, 58
goals, 14
hippocampus, 97–103
hormones, 100–102
images, 44–45, 47–48
JFK, 1–4, 7–9, 19–22, 44, 81–82, 87, 120, 125
limbic system, 95–103
'live' quality, 3, 4, 6, 59
long-term potentiation, 103–105, 121
Margaret Thatcher, 53–66, 120
memory consistency, 22, 33, 38, 40, 47, 77–78
narrative conventions, 18, 25–26
news public/events/items, 1–3, 6, 9–10, 15, 22–23, 32, 39–40, 50, 63, 67, 90
"Now Print!", 13–14, 96, 107
Pearl Harbour, 20–22, 82
personal circumstances, 3, 24, 37
personal importance/significance. 5, 9, 11, 23–24, 32, 41, 54, 60–65, 68–70, 74, 81, 90–92, 109, 114–117
plans, 117–122
prior knowledge, 14–15, 60–65
private/Personal experiences, 3, 27, 49, 50, 52
PTSD, 80–81, 112

questionnaire, 27–29, 33–39, 44, 48–49, 53, 70–73, 87
rating/rating scale, 5, 9, 27–29, 30–31, 39, 54, 68, 77
reception event, 5–6, 10–14, 18, 25, 28, 30, 37–40, 47–48, 54, 58, 82
reconstruction, 19, 21–23, 37–38, 59, 81, 111
rehearsal, 5, 9, 17–23, 26, 29, 30, 32, 44–49, 60–65, 72, 90–92
remindings/other memories, 48, 61
retention interval, 27, 33–39, 43–47, 54, 74–75
retest, 27, 33–39, 43–49, 53–57, 74
Ronald Reagan, 43–47
self, 15, 21, 76, 81, 91
source monitoring, 19, 22, 35
surprise/surprising, 1, 9–15, 19–27, 31–40, 47–48, 53, 67–76, 82, 84, 114–117
traumatic events, 76–81, 86–87, 90–91
TV focus, 29, 37, 57
vivid(ness)/clarity, 1, 3–4, 29, 33, 37, 45–48, 68, 70–75, 79, 87, 90–92, 114
'wrong time slice' errors, 35–36, 58, 59